LifespanDoulas

DONA Birth Doula Workshop
Class Manual

By Patty Brennan

These materials have been authored by Patty Brennan unless indicated otherwise. Doulas who have completed training through Lifespan Doulas, LLC are welcome to use any of these materials with their doula clients. You do not have permission to reproduce these materials for use in childbirth classes or other classes/trainings that you may develop, nor do you have permission to share these materials with other doulas. For more information on trainings by Patty Brennan, see www.LifespanDoulas.com or email patty@LifespanDoulas.com.

ISBN 978-1717563187

Table of Contents

Daily Schedule

Friday, 8:30am–6pm

Nutrition and Discomforts of Pregnancy
Hormones of Labor
Stages of Labor Overview (videos)

Lunch (1–2 pm)

Facilitating Informed Decision Making
Communicating with Care Providers
Pain Coping Exercise
Values Clarification

Saturday, 8:30am–6pm

The Meaning of Support
DONA International Scope of Practice
Professional Boundaries
DONA International Certification Process

Lunch (1–2pm)

Gate Control Theory of Pain
Relaxation, Rhythm & Ritual
Active Labor ~ The Doula's Role
Comfort Measures
Use of the Peanut Ball
Touch in Labor
Positioning for Labor

Sunday, 8:30am–5pm

Early Labor ~ The Doula's Role
2nd Stage of Labor ~ The Doula's Role
3rd State of Labor
Posterior Presentation ~ Prevention, Correction & Support Techniques
Visit from a Birth Doula

Lunch (12:30–1:30pm)

Holding Space ~ Immediate Postpartum Recovery
Labor & Birth Role Play
Cesarean Birth ~ The Doula's Role
Supporting the Partner
The Birth Doula's Role Postpartum
Closing & Workshop Evaluation

Discomforts and Complications of Pregnancy
Answer Key

Anemia (5)
- Decrease in total amount of red blood cells or hemoglobin in the blood, or lowered ability of the blood to carry oxygen
- Caused by expansion of blood volume in pregnancy accompanied by a lack of sufficient iron in diet
- Shortness of breath on exertion, e.g., huffing and puffing when climbing stairs
- Prevent by eating iron-rich foods
- Corrected by taking iron supplements (beware of constipation caused by some iron supplements)

Constipation (7)
- Failure to have at least one bowel movement per day and/or straining to pass bowel movements
- May be accompanied by headaches as body reabsorbs toxins from the lower bowel
- Caused by relaxation of smooth muscle in the body, including muscle in the intestinal track (one of the effects of the hormone progesterone)
- Caused by dehydration
- Caused by poor-quality iron supplements (also turn the stool black)
- Repeat straining may cause hemorrhoids (varicose veins of the rectum) or exacerbate existing hemorrhoids
- Corrections include drink more fluids; quit iron supplements that body can't digest; add more fruits and veggies to the diet; exercise more; raise feet on small stool when passing a bowel movement (aids elimination without straining); prunes/prune juice

Edema (7)
- Fluids leak out of blood stream into interstitial tissues, causing swelling
- Most commonly seen in ankles and feet, but can be systemic (noticeable in hands, face)
- When this symptom appears in conjunction with high blood pressure and protein in the urine, mother may have pre-eclampsia
- "Pitting" occurs when a thumb is pressed into the swollen tissues and the tissue holds the thumbprint for several seconds after releasing pressure.
- Symptoms made worse from dehydration (body thinks it should hold onto the fluid it has)
- Symptoms improved by drinking fluids (body starts to dump excess fluids)
- Sudden and severe onset of symptoms indicates a need for immediate call to care provider

Hypoglycemia (5)

- Low blood sugar
- Symptoms include drop in energy level, urgent hunger, nausea, light-headed, fainting
- Symptoms made worse by over-consumption of sugar and empty calories that are high in carbohydrates (aka "junk food")
- Symptoms improved by eating high-protein snacks
- Symptoms improved by eating more frequent, smaller meals throughout the day

Indigestion, heartburn (8)

- Food digests more slowly or digestion is distressful
- Stomach acids back up into the esophagus, causing a burning sensation
- Caused by relaxation of smooth muscle in the body, including muscle in the intestinal track (one of the effects of the hormone progesterone); the pyloric sphincter relaxes
- Helped by eating smaller, more frequent meals throughout the day
- Helped by eating lightly in the evening, before lying down (and/or try resting with upper torso slightly elevate)
- Going for a walk after dinner may help.
- Avoid foods that exacerbate the problem (pay attention to patterns)
- Try chewing a few papaya enzyme tablets or a small handful of raw cashews or almonds for relief. (Tums have aluminum in them, which is toxic, and while it is true that Tums contain calcium, it is not an easily absorbed source of calcium.)

Insomnia (5)

- Changing biorhythm prepares mother for life with a newborn
- May be caused by frequent urination, leg cramps, hip pain, etc.
- Brainstorm strategies to aid comfort and relaxation
- Encourage mom not to worry about it; go with the flow
- Encourage mom to investigate flexing her work hours around her sleep needs or arranging to quit working well before her due date

Low Backache (7)

- Achy, tired feeling in the lower back and sacral area
- Due to growth of baby and strain on uterine ligaments attached at the sacrum
- Due to shift in body's center of gravity, leading to a sway-back position which further strains the ligaments
- Symptoms worse when abdominal muscles are weak, untoned
- Pelvic rock exercise provides relief
- Maternity belt or girdle may provide support/relief
- Beware that if the backache is intermittent, it may be caused by uterine contractions and could be a sign of labor (including premature labor)

Muscle cramping (calf muscles, uterine irritability, spasms) (5)
- Caused by dehydration
- Caused by a lack of absorbable dietary calcium
- Potassium levels may be low
- Drink more fluids
- Eat a banana

Pica (pronounced "py-ka") (5)
- Craving for non-food items (e.g., clay, dirt, chalk, ice shavings, smell of gasoline, etc.)
- Mom may feel embarrassed and reluctant to report her symptoms
- Caused by pronounced lack of minerals in the diet
- Dietary counseling is in order
- Symptoms improve with high-quality (all natural, easily absorbed) mineral supplement

Premature Labor (5)
- Onset of labor prior to 37 weeks gestation
- More common with a first baby
- Increased risk if you have had this happen with a previous pregnancy
- May be caused by dehydration
- Mom should get off her feet, drink a pint of fluid, and call her care provider

Varicose veins (8)
- Weakness in the wall of a vein where the vessel becomes large and twisted; may appear as a blue bulge
- Often manifest in the legs during pregnancy, but may also manifest in the vagina, on the vulva, or in the rectum
- Inherited weakness/tendency; runs in families
- Never really go away, but will be worse during pregnancy due to increased blood volume and circulation challenges from growing weight of baby in utero
- Symptoms worse from long periods of standing (gravity causing blood to pool in lower extremities) or too much sitting (compressing return blood flow at the groin)
- Varicose veins of rectum (aka "hemorrhoids") may be made worse from pushing during 2nd stage of labor
- Dietary counseling, herbs, homeopathy, therapeutic yoga poses and other complementary therapies may help prevent the problem or, when present, help prevent symptoms from worsening.
- Witch hazel compresses can be applied for pain relief

- not about treating the discomforts, more about normalizing

Summary of Key Points
Nutrition and Discomforts of Pregnancy

Discomforts of pregnancy
- Many are related to normal physiological changes in the body.
- Many are preventable through proper nutrition.
- Food cravings indicate an attempt at self-correction. Pay attention to the cravings and learn to read them properly.
- Kidneys and liver are working overtime to purify the bloodstream of toxins for both mom and baby.

Drink more fluids
- To support adequate expansion of blood volume
- To prevent problems such as constipation, edema, and even premature labor
- Fluid Intake Rule: Body weight divided by two = the number of fluid ounces needed per day

More protein is needed
- To sustain energy levels throughout the day
- To support adequate expansion of blood volume
- Limit meats with excessive quantities of preservatives

Increased need for minerals
- Iron needed to create red blood cells that circulate oxygen in the expanded bloodstream
- Calcium needed because baby will leach needed calcium from mother's bones; pregnancy will deplete her unless diet provides what baby requires
- Lack of bio-available minerals connected to numerous complaints of pregnancy

Good-quality fats are needed
- Support optimal brain growth for baby
- Help digest protein
- Slow absorption of carbohydrates, preventing high blood sugar peaks
- Help support normal elasticity of tissues (prevent stretch marks, tearing of perineum at birth)
- Satisfying, makes food taste good

Carbohydrates
- Emphasize fresh fruits, vegetables, and whole grains.
- Balanced with protein and good-quality fats, will help sustain energy levels throughout the day
- Limit empty calories, junk foods

Implications for Doulas
- Help mom make connections between choices and consequences; use as motivation for change.
- Help mom identify strategies to meet her own needs.

Optimizing Your Prenatal Nutrition

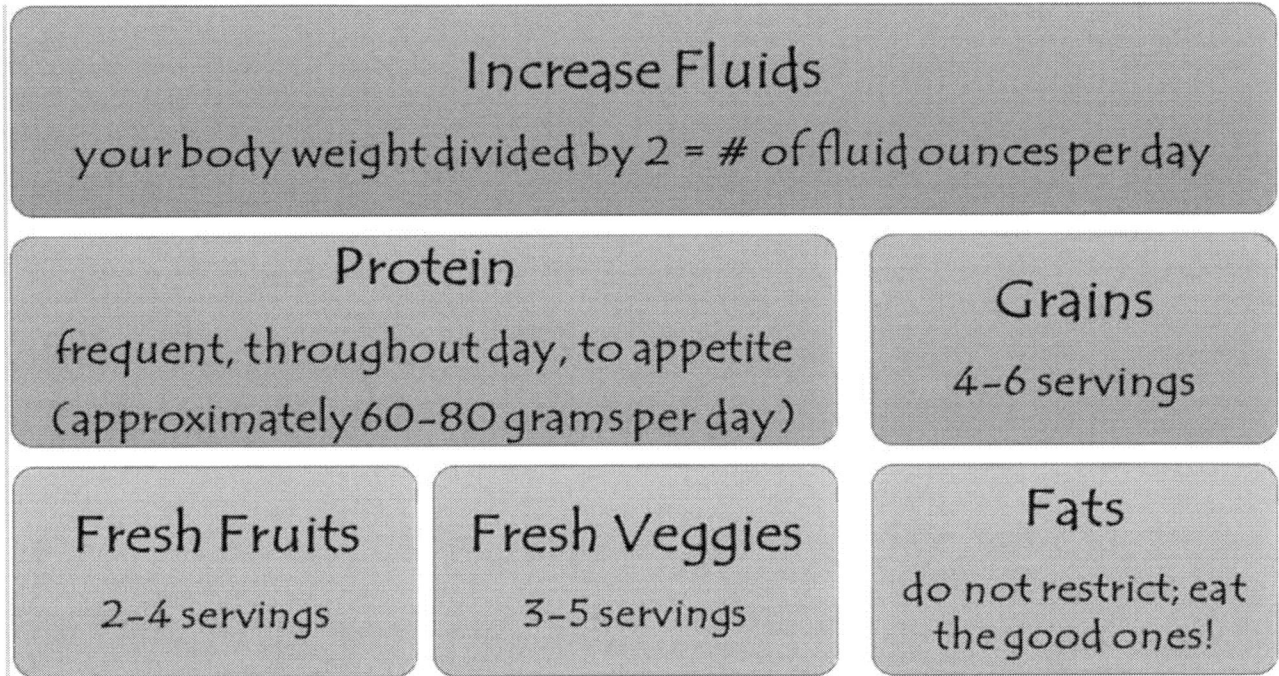

> ## Increase Fluids
> your body weight divided by 2 = # of fluid ounces per day

> ## Protein
> frequent, throughout day, to appetite (approximately 60-80 grams per day)

> ## Grains
> 4-6 servings

> ## Fresh Fruits
> 2-4 servings

> ## Fresh Veggies
> 3-5 servings

> ## Fats
> do not restrict; eat the good ones!

Good Fluid Choices: water, Pregnancy Tea, herbal tea, 100% fruit juice
Limit: coffee, caffeinated tea, pop
Avoid: alcohol, diet pop, drinks with high fructose corn syrup

Good Protein Choices: red meats, whole turkey breast, chicken, legumes, nuts and seeds, dairy, eggs, tofu, fish and seafood; eat organic if possible; eat high protein snacks
Limit: lunch meats and other foods loaded with preservatives
Avoid: Fish and seafood high in mercury and other heavy metals

Eat High-Quality Fats: olive oil, coconut oil, flax seed oil, butter, whole milk dairy products, avocados, nuts and seeds, high-fat fish and seafood, lard
Avoid: hydrogenated fats, margarine, rancid fats

Eat a Wide Variety of Fresh Fruits and Veggies: if not fresh, frozen is next best choice; the deeper the color, the higher the vitamin and mineral content (e.g., dark leafy greens are better than iceberg lettuce); organic if possible
Limit: dried fruits and fruit juices—both are high in sugar

Eat Whole Grains Everyday: brown rice, oatmeal, millet, buckwheat, whole grain breads, etc.
Limit: white flour products (white bread, pasta, pastries, etc.), white rice, high carb treats with refined white sugar, junk food
Avoid: empty calories with artificial ingredients

Condiments and Such:
Good dressings: high-quality oils and a variety of vinegars (balsamic, cider vinegar, etc.); or mix fresh lemon juice and olive oil with a bit of Dijon mustard
Good additions: kelp powder, sea salt, apple cider vinegar
Good natural sweeteners: maple syrup, honey, molasses
Limit: refined white sugar
Avoid: artificial sweeteners in any form (e.g., diet pop)

Tips for the Busy Working Pregnant Woman

✓ Quality over quantity
✓ Never go hungry
✓ Eat more frequently
✓ Plan ahead
✓ Have high-protein snacks available

---

prevent tearing: lots of water, fatty foods/ proteins, flax seed/vitamin E oil on perineum... also eat flax seed

Common Discomforts of Pregnancy and
Alternatives to Drugs for Relief

The following is a guide to the common discomforts of pregnancy, their causes and cures. Generally, aches and pains are reduced by good muscle tone, as there is then less strain on ligaments and joints. Women should keep up some regular form of exercise and practice good body mechanics in standing, sitting, rising, walking, climbing, reaching, lifting, etc. Walking and swimming are excellent, especially if you were not already exercising regularly prior to becoming pregnant. Adequate rest and a well-balanced diet also minimize discomforts.

Leg Cramps

Cause
- pressure of uterus on blood vessels, lessening the flow of blood to the legs
- overextension of the foot; occurs with pointing of the toes (e.g., when bedcovers are too heavy, with tightly made bed, or when exercises are improperly done)
- sudden stretching
- fatigue or chilling
- lack of calcium in diet
- excessive amounts of phosphorus absorbed from milk and milk products, which impede the absorption of calcium

Relief
- stretch the cramped muscle, improving circulation; stretch should be gentle and constant, not jerky
- for foot cramp, stand on affected foot
- for cramp in calf, straighten the knee, flex the foot, hold, then relax and repeat if necessary
- for cramp in front of thigh, stretch leg backward
- for cramp in buttock, stretch leg forward
- NEVER massage a cramped muscle; it enhances the cramp
- try adding more calcium to your diet; sesame seeds, dark leafy greens, and pregnancy tea are excellent non-dairy sources
- soak in an Epsom Salts bath

Groin Aches or Pains

Cause
- poor posture
- standing too long
- pressure of baby
- spasm of round ligaments

Relief
- do light effleurage (small circular massage) in groin area, giving a slight lift as hands come upward; do not use pressure on the down stroke

- for relief of sudden spasm, pull up leg on same side as spasm, as if tying a shoe, or lie down on affected side with leg drawn up
- try applying heat via a hot water bottle, heating pad or rice soak; or soak in a hot with Epsom Salts bath

Ache in Back, Hips, or Thighs

Cause
- pressure of baby on small nerves inside of vertebrae and pelvis
- shift in mother's center of gravity with accompanying poor posture; more common in multiparas with poor muscle tone; lax abdominal muscles let uterus fall forward, leading to poor posture for maintenance of balance
- softening effect of hormones on connective tissue of spine and sacroiliac joints

Relief
- pelvic rock on all fours
- careful attention to correct posture and body mechanics
- when standing, lift one foot and place it on an object so it is higher than the other foot; or stand with one foot in front of the other and rock back and forth slightly
- try a prenatal yoga class
- firm mattress
- chiropractic adjustment may help if what you are feeling is pain rather than ache or stress, or if the problem is chronic
- sciatica, or shooting pain from the buttock down the leg, may be relieved by elevating the legs in a right-angle position against the wall
- take care when driving; use a pillow behind your back; adjust the car seat; stretch often on long rides

Caution: Be careful not to classify all backaches as to the same cause. Find the exact location and type of pain. Backache waist-high and to one side may indicate kidney problems. Ache in the middle of a buttock with muscle cramping may be due to a sacroiliac problem. Rhythmic lower back pain could be labor.

Fingers (tingling, numbness, swelling)

Cause
- enlargement of breast tissue high in armpit, resulting in pressure on nerves and blood vessels

Relief
- place hands on shoulders and rotate elbows in a circle

Diaphragm Pressure (cramp or stitch under ribs)

Cause
- baby high in abdomen, compressing the diaphragm against the base of the lungs

Relief
- lift rib cage by raising arms sideways and upward above the head; stretch

Dyspnea (shortness of breath)

Cause
- baby high in abdomen, compressing the diaphragm against the base of the lungs
- may indicate anemia

Relief
- sleep propped up with pillows or spend first ten minutes in bed lying on back with arms extended above head and resting back on the bed
- relief occurs later in the pregnancy when the baby engages, or moves deeper in the pelvis
- if anemia is the problem, increase natural sources of iron in diet (raisins, blackstrap molasses, wheat germ, kelp, apricots, and leafy greens – especially kale, Swiss chard, mustard and turnip greens); drink lots of Pregnancy Tea; Floradix Herbs Plus Iron is a natural iron supplement available at health food stores

Dizziness, Fainting, Lightheadedness

Cause
- vasomotor changes
- pressure of uterus on greater abdominal vessels
- anemia
- hypoglycemia

Relief
- avoid sudden changes in posture; after lying down, get up slowly, rolling to one side, then slowly push up to a sitting position using your arms
- follow advice regarding anemia above
- do not skip meals; eat good food frequently
- avoid hot, stuffy rooms

Heartburn

Cause
- enlarged uterus displaces stomach upward
- hormones relax cardiac sphincter of stomach, slow digestion, and allow stomach acids to back up into esophagus
- nervous tension, worry and fatigue intensify problem

Relief
- eat several small meals a day instead of three large ones
- avoid greasy or highly spiced foods and coffee
- if problem is especially bad at night, sleep propped up with pillows; don't lie down right after eating

- avoid over-the-counter remedies, especially baking soda and Alka-Seltzer because of their high sodium content; some antacids contain aluminum which is toxic; others contain poorly assimilated calcium
- try papaya enzyme tablets, umeboshi plum balls, raw almonds or raw cashews (a few, chewed to a pulp)
- gently massaging the stomach downward may help
- a reflexology (foot massage) treatment may help

Constipation

Cause
- diet poor in fiber
- diminished peristalsis due to pressure of enlarged uterus and the relaxing effect of hormones on the smooth muscles of the intestines
- excess iron from prenatal vitamins which the body can't assimilate; turns the stool black

Relief
- drink more fluids, especially in the morning to aid elimination
- increase intake of fiber; have at least two servings of whole grains (real oatmeal, brown rice, millet, barley, etc.) daily and increase your intake of fresh, raw fruits and vegetables
- make sure diet contains plenty of B vitamins found in wheat germ, whole grains and Brewer's yeast
- walk more
- when sitting on toilet, put feet up on a small stool; relax pelvic floor
- abandon poor-quality vitamins or iron pills and search for iron-rich foods or high-quality food-grown vitamins; drink Pregnancy Tea
- if problem persists, consult your midwife for herbal or homeopathic help and then discover a preventive maintenance plan (such as an apple and brown rice each day, or prunes at night, etc.); it is extremely important to not be constipated during pregnancy

Hemorrhoids (varicose veins of the lower bowel and rectum)

Cause
- relaxing effect of progesterone and pressure of heavy uterus on lower part of large bowel
- obesity
- lack of exercise, excessive sitting
- constipation
- straining to move bowels

Relief
- same as for constipation
- do pelvic floor exercises (Kegels) regularly to simulate circulation in the pelvic area
- apply cold compresses (e.g., ice, witch hazel)
Pregnancy Tea to tone the vascular system

Varicose Veins

Cause
- hereditary predisposition
- relaxing effect of progesterone on walls of veins
- pressure of enlarged uterus on abdominal veins slows blood return from lower limbs, so blood tends to pool in the weakened veins
- fatigue
- standing with knees locked, causing muscular constriction which prevents proper venous return
- standing or sitting in one position for a long period of time

Relief
- avoid round garters, thigh highs, or any clothing that causes constriction and pressure on any part of the body
- change positions frequently; avoid long standing or sitting without relief
- take walks regularly; the massaging action of muscles close to veins is good for stimulating circulation
- elevate legs several times a day; the more severe the problem, the more frequent the elevation; lie on floor with legs straight up the wall as though sitting on the wall; relax for a few minutes
- wear support hose or stockings made of elastic; put on while lying down, ideally before getting up in the morning
- never stand "at attention" with knees locked; they should always be slightly flexed
- Vitamin E capsules may aid circulation and bring some relief (do not exceed 600 IU per day)
- drink Pregnancy Tea; add Rose Hips for the bioflavonoids
- Rutin, a part of the vitamin C complex, can be taken in capsule form, after the first trimester
- for varicosities of the vulva, lie with hips elevated several times a day

The Process of Labor and Birth
Summary Sheet

Pre-Labor Changes

Changes in Late Pregnancy (last four weeks or so):
- Baby engages ("drops") in the pelvis. For first-time mothers, this typically happens approximately two weeks prior to birth, though it can be weeks prior or even wait until labor has begun. For a second or more baby, engagement can happen any time.
- Mom may feel increased pressure on her bladder; pressure on diaphragm is relieved; sometimes pubic bone feels sore.
- Emotionally, mom may be feeling discouraged, anxious, excited, tired of being pregnant, etc.
- Cervix begins to soften, ripen and move forward, typically any time after 36 weeks.
- Cervix may begin to efface (thin) and dilate (open).

Signs of Impending Labor (one day or two prior to onset of labor):
- Frequent, loose bowel movements (may also accompany onset of contractions)
- Nesting instinct with sense of urgency regarding chores, errands, purchases that must happen *NOW*. (Note to partners: this is not necessarily a rational process; just go with it.)

First Stage of Labor (Effacement and Dilation of Cervix)

Three ways for labor to begin:
1. Bloody show: mucus plug dislodges from the cervix; because there are capillaries in the cervix and the cervix is changing, the mucus is likely to be tinged with blood; may or may not be accompanied by noticeable contractions.
2. Contractions: the pattern here can be pretty much anything from one per hour lasting 15 seconds, to every 10 minutes, lasting 30 seconds or more; endless variations; may or may not be accompanied by bloody show; contractions may feel like menstrual cramps or may be felt in the low back as an intermittent backache; contractions do not go away when mom changes her position or activity level; most women report that labor contractions feel "different" than the toning contractions of late pregnancy (aka "Braxton-Hicks contractions"). The term "false labor" is used when a woman experiences contractions that are regular for a time but disappear altogether when she changes her position or activity level.
3. Spontaneous Rupture of Membranes (SROM): bag of water breaks and fluid gushes from the vagina; can also be experienced as a slow leak which may be hard to differentiate from urine leakage (not terribly uncommon in late pregnancy with weight of baby directly on top of the bladder); care provider can determine the difference with simple office visit to check pH of fluid that is present; expect differences among care providers regarding willingness to wait for labor contractions to begin on their own once SROM

has occurred; note whether or not the fluid is clear or has a brownish-green tint to it; if it is not clear, then the baby has passed meconium in utero (the first bowel movement) indicating a need to monitor the baby more closely in labor. SROM is the first sign of labor in about 10 percent of women; it is more typical for the bag of waters to break later in the birth process (>7cm dilation).

Early Labor:
- Cervix continues to ripen, efface, move forward and begins dilating.
- Contractions progress, possibly with bloody show and/or rupture of membranes.
- Contractions get longer and stronger and closer together.
- Mom may feel excited, confident, optimistic, anxious, performance anxiety….
- Mom can talk through contractions and do other activities between contractions.
- Mom may focus more than necessary on the contractions.

  What to do?
  - Check the instructions your doctor/midwife/doula has given you regarding when they want to be notified if you think you are in labor and follow those instructions; medical caregiver will advise when it is time to come in; doula may join you at home or at the hospital.
  - If membranes are ruptured, do not put anything inside the vagina; be careful about hygiene (keeping bacteria from the rectum away from vaginal opening); refrain from tub baths until you are in active labor.
  - An adrenaline rush often accompanies onset of labor; remind mom to save this energy for the hard work that is to come; help her to relax, deep breathing, warm bath if membranes are intact, etc.
  - If at night: SLEEP (or at least rest)!
  - Eat, drink, empty bladder frequently. VERY IMPORTANT!
  - Alternate distracting activities (bath, music, walk, cards, reading, movie, computer games) with rest if tired.
  - When contractions become more regular, time them for a while (4 or 5 at a time, every few hours or when labor seems to have changed).

more like 6 cm now ←

Active Phase (4–8 cm dilation):
- Cervix is now 100% effaced and 4 cm dilated.
- Contractions continuing to get longer and stronger and closer together, typically coming 3–5 minutes apart and lasting at least 1 minute.
- Mom's attention is increasingly drawn inward; no longer distractible; the labor has become everything—getting through one contraction at a time, recovering and getting ready for the next contraction.
- Mom is working hard; may be sweating and breathing differently; can no longer talk through a contraction; she may be tensing during contractions.
- Cervix continues dilating and baby's head begins to rotate as he/she moves deeper in the pelvis.
- May continue to see bloody show or bag of waters may rupture anytime.

- "Moment of truth;" mom may feel trapped, discouraged, recognizing labor is not within her control.
- May resent disturbances and interruptions.
- May want pain medications. If not, then natural pain management techniques and comfort measures can be used.

<u>What to do?</u>
- o When the shift happens to active labor, you may want to head to the hospital/birth center or have your midwife on her way to you (for homebirth).
- o In any case, doula (or other support team members) should join you now.
- o Drink fluids and keep bladder empty.
- o Help mom with relaxation; begin coping ritual.
- o Provide relief with comfort measures.
- o "Labor voice," murmuring soothing, encouraging words.

Transition (8–10 cm):
- Contractions are very close, peak intensity (1–2 minutes apart, lasting approximately 1.5 minutes); contractions may piggyback.
- Mom may vomit.
- Mom may get lost in the intensity of the labor; feel afraid or panicky.
- Mom may scream, thrash, tense, weep, or protest; she is likely to say she "can't go on," "how much longer?" and so on.
- Bloody show may be present, or rupture of membranes may occur.
- Mom may start to feel "pushy."

<u>What to do?</u>
- o Move in close, establish eye contact and provide minute-to-minute support.
- o Remind her that this is the shortest phase of labor.
- o Hang in there!

The Rest and Be Thankful Phase of Labor (10 cm dilated):
- For some women, labor can slow down at complete dilation.
- This resting phase is often not acknowledged by some care providers who may call for Pitocin or encourage voluntary pushing efforts.
- Mom may experience relief, renewed energy, enthusiasm, hope, or readiness to "get on with it."

<u>What to do?</u>
- o Empty bladder now, before pushing efforts begin.
- o Drink, maybe something with a little sweetness to it (cup of hot tea with a generous spoonful of honey).
- o Negotiate with care provider regarding letting labor unfold at its own pace.
- o Help mom get comfortable, dark room, quiet.
- o Rest!

2nd Stage of Labor (Descent and Birth of Baby)

Descent Phase:
- Contractions are 3–5 minutes apart and lasting about 1 minute, perhaps a little longer.
- Mom may feel an urge to push with contractions.
- Mom may feel rectal pressure, as though she must pass a bowel movement.
- Mom may spontaneously hold her breath for part of a contraction or make deep grunting sounds.
- Baby rotates and descends.
- It may take a few contractions for mom to get her new rhythm and feel effective with pushing.
- As baby makes it under the pubic bone, the head may start to be visible at the vaginal opening; a little more with each contraction but disappearing between contractions.
- Mom may try to pull away from/resist sensation of pressure and stretching as baby moves down.
- Mom may pass stool during this phase, as the baby compresses the lower bowel.
- Nurse or midwife is in the room now, until the birth; if OB is attending, they will likely come in close to the end while the L&D nurse will be attending you during most of 2nd stage.
- Caregiver may be doing coached or directed pushing.

  What to do?
  - Encourage mom to try different upright positions (especially if progress is slow).
  - Keep breathing and use lower (not high-pitched) sounds.
  - "Down and out." "Let the baby come."
  - If a lot of stool is passing, or mom is especially concerned about it, see if she can do some pushing on the toilet for a while.
  - Provide physical support for positioning, if needed.
  - Encourage her and give her progress reports; if mom wants to see, set up a mirror for her, or encourage her to reach down and touch her baby's head, or tell her when you can first see the baby's head.
  - Keep offering fluids.
  - Cool wash cloths to face and neck, between contractions.
  - Remind caregiver regarding any points in your Birth Plan related to episiotomy or immediate post-birth care (e.g., delayed cord clamping, skin-to-skin).

Crowning and Birth:
- Head no longer rocks back and forth, but remains visible at vaginal opening, even between contractions.
- Mom feels a burning sensation as baby's head stretches her tissues.
- Caregiver may do episiotomy at this time.
- Caregiver (OB or midwife) is calling the shots at this time.
- As the head emerges, baby rotates and then the shoulders birth one at a time, followed by the rest of the baby's body.

- Baby may be placed directly on mom's belly, with the cord intact (recommended), or the cord may be severed, and baby removed to warming table for routine procedures.

<u>What to do?</u>
  - o When mom feels "the burn," help her slow down pushing efforts by panting; as long as the breath is going in and out, she is not pushing; establish eye contact if necessary to help her with this; keep the breath in the upper chest.
  - o Care provider applies a little counter pressure to perineum, oil, hot compresses, if desired.
  - o Remind doctor/midwife of pertinent requests in Birth Plan (especially regarding episiotomy, cord cutting if requesting delay).

3rd Stage (Delivery of the Placenta)
- Contractions continue, though with much less discomfort.
- As the uterus gets smaller and smaller, the placenta no longer has a surface area to be attached to and it is released from the uterine wall, followed by a gush of blood.
- Attendant will encourage mom to push out her placenta.
- Once the placenta has been delivered, the nurse/midwife will periodically check the uterus for firmness, to ensure that it stays contracted in order to shut off blood vessels at the site and control bleeding.
- Baby is either skin-to-skin with mom (recommended) or under heat lamp in container, typically a few feet from the bed.
- Putting baby to breast releases oxytocin, which helps the uterus to contract.

<u>What to do?</u>
  - o Continue to advocate for your Birth Plan.
  - o Allow the baby access to the breast.

Immediate Postpartum Period (first 2 hours)
- Some moms may get "the shakes."
- Continue bonding/breastfeeding.
- Routine medical procedures for newborn (weighing, Vitamin K, eye prophylaxis, newborn bath).
- Nurse/midwife stays close at hand and monitors mom's bleeding and baby's vital sign.
- Mom helped up to bathroom, to keep bladder empty.
- Mom washed up a bit or an herbal bath is drawn for mom and baby (homebirth, some birth centers).
- Meal for mom and partner.

<u>What to do?</u>
  - o Warm mom with blankets.
  - o Continue to advocate for your Birth Plan (perhaps delaying non-critical newborn procedures for an hour or two).
  - o Take pictures; make phone calls; receive visitors, if desired.
  - o Celebrate! Rest.

Immediate Postpartum Period after Cesarean Delivery

- Mom will go to post-op recovery room with partner. Baby will accompany, provided baby has not been transferred to a Special Care Nursery or the Neonatal Intensive Care Unit (NICU).
- Other visitors may be allowed in at this time.
- If baby is in NICU, dad/partner may want to stay with the baby; doula or other support team member stays with mom until she is stable enough to be brought to baby.
- Mom may have "the shakes." Some women feel nauseated from the anesthesia after surgery. Anti-nausea medications may be given.
- Usually good pain control is still in place from the epidural.
- Once stable, mom and baby are moved to a postpartum room; may go back to room you which you were laboring in some hospitals.

What to do?

- o If baby is with you, enjoy your baby, skin-to-skin, near the breast; baby may root and latch on his/her own; just provide access.
- o Continue to advocate for any parts of your Birth Plan involving after-birth care.
- o If dad/partner is with the baby elsewhere, touch your baby if possible; talk to your baby; call your baby by name; let the baby know you are there.
- o If mom and baby are separated, have a support person relay information (and pictures!) of baby to mom; back and forth, until they are together.
- o Take pictures, make calls, receive visitors if desired.
- o Celebrate! Rest.

Active Management of Third Stage of Labor

Definitions and Related Facts

Postpartum hemorrhage and complications of third stage of labor
- Blood loss in excess of 500 ml, with severe postpartum hemorrhage being loss of 1,000 ml or more, and very severe being a loss of 2,500 ml or more.
- Anemia in the mother can pre-exist or be the result of hemorrhage; severe cases may necessitate a blood transfusion.
- Postpartum hemorrhage is the main cause of maternal death in a number of countries, the vast majority of which occur in the developing world.

Active management of third stage
- 10 units IM Pitocin administered to all mothers within one minute of delivery.
- Early clamping and cutting of the umbilical cord, often before the cord ceases to pulse (thereby cutting off the transfer to the baby of his/her full blood volume).
- Wait one minute, after clamping the cord, and initiate controlled cord traction for delivery of the placenta.

Expectant management of third stage
- Signs of placental separation are awaited, and the placenta is delivered spontaneously via normal uterine contractions.
- May involve nipple stimulation by putting the baby to breast immediately after delivery, stimulating an oxytocin surge in the mother.
- Medical interventions that interfere with the body's natural oxytocin release may reduce the effectiveness of the physiological process (i.e., oxytocin release can be inhibited by anxiety and excess adrenaline, oxytocin augmentation in labor, and administration of epidural or narcotic analgesia).
- The umbilical cord is left intact until it has ceased pulsing and baby has received his/her full blood volume.
- Uterotonic drugs are used only in cases of excess bleeding.

What does the evidence say?

Medical recommendations in favor of active management over expectant management of third stage of labor are based on an updated Cochrane Review of seven studies involving 8,247 women. For all women, irrespective of their risk of severe bleeding, active management protocols reduced the incidence of severe postpartum blood loss, maternal blood transfusions and postpartum anemia. At the same time, the following statistically significant negative effects of active management were noted:

- Increase in mother's blood pressure, afterpains, vomiting and use of drugs for pain relief; these effects are apparently due to administration of a specific uterotonic (choice of drug used, specifically ergometrine).

- Increase in the number of women returning to the hospital ER after discharge (between 24 hours and up to 6 weeks) due to bleeding (3.8% of patients requiring additional treatment in the active management group vs. 3.1% in the expectant management group).
- Decrease in newborn birth weight due to early cord clamping leading to a 20% reduction in the baby's overall blood volume. *(The World Health Organization now recommends active management with delayed cord clamping—allowing baby's blood that is in the placenta to return to the baby's circulation—to reduce the likelihood of anemia in the newborn. However, in many healthcare settings, this recommendation is not followed.)*

Discussion by Authors

"The previous authors of this review [2011] recommended active management of the third stage due to the benefit identified in terms of reduced incidence of severe bleeding. We agree that bleeding is a very important component when balancing the benefits and harms of active compared to expectant management of the third stage of labor. However, we consider that the number of harms caused by active management also deserve consideration. In particular, the increased rate of hypertension, increased numbers of mothers returning to hospital due to bleeding and the possible decrease in average blood volume of newborns reflected in the lower birthweight for babies where the mother has received active management of the third stage, are of concern. *In the population of women at low risk of bleeding such harms are of more concern as there was no statistical evidence that severe bleeding was reduced by active management.*" [Emphasis added.]

Authors' Conclusions

"Healthcare providers should, therefore, present information to all women in the antenatal period on the advantages and disadvantages of both methods of third-stage management to facilitate their discussion and informed choice of care. This information should include not only the benefits of active management … but also the harms to the mother … In addition, information regarding the effects on the baby of early versus deferred cord clamping should be provided…."

Source
Cochrane Review, *Active versus expectant management for women in the third stage of labor.* Cochrane Library 2015 Issue 3.

Commentary

Question for Parents to Consider. For low-risk women, especially those experiencing drug free labors, do the benefits of active management of third stage of labor outweigh the risks? *Parents are encouraged to discuss the benefits and risks of active management with their midwife or doctor as it applies uniquely to their situation.*

Things Are Happening Fast and Informed Consent. In my experience, in healthcare settings where active management is routine, informed consent for this practice is rare. Two specific pieces of active management—early cord clamping and administration of Pitocin— are usually completed within a minute after birth. Therefore, many parents (being somewhat distracted) may not even notice what is being done until after the fact. Parents who prefer an expectant management approach will need to discuss their preferences with their care provider, express their wishes in a birth plan and then be prepared to advocate for their preferences at the birth. Keep in mind that whomever you discussed this with prenatally is not necessarily the same person who will be attending your birth.

Mixed Management Option. Further study is needed on the possibility of a "mixed management option" but should be considered based on the mother's risk factors. A mixed management system might be most beneficial for someone with a high-risk birth. For example, for someone with low iron, one option might look like this: IM Pitocin immediately following the birth to decrease the chance of hemorrhage (active management), delayed cord clamping to allow the baby to receive his/her full blood volume from the placenta (expectant management), and careful cord traction once the cord is done pulsing to ensure there isn't excessive bleeding behind the placenta (mild active management).

Delayed Cord Clamping. In a post on Lamaze International's *Science and Sensibility* blog, pediatrician Dr. Mark Sloan examines common objections to delayed cord clamping and what the evidence says about its benefits. Dr. Sloan concludes, *"The evidence of benefit from delayed cord clamping is so compelling that the burden of proof must now lie with those who wish to continue the practice of immediate clamping, rather than with those who prefer—as nature intended—to wait."*

Prevent Anemia. If active management of third stage is being promoted as a benefit to anemic mothers (those with low blood levels of iron who might suffer more from even a normal blood loss at their birth), then let's become as proactive as possible about preventing and treating anemia prior to the birth through proper nutrition and supplementation.

The Midwifery Model of Care. Finally, in my opinion, active management of third stage of labor is inconsistent with the Midwifery Model of Care [www.cfmidwifery.org]. Specifically, it violates the basic tenet of respect for the birth process as it unfolds uniquely, as well as the belief that birth is a normal life process for which women's bodies are well designed. This is to be distinguished from the medical model approach wherein birth is viewed as an emergency waiting to happen and interference with the normal process is common.

Models of Childbirth
By Amy L. Gilliland, Ph.D., BDT(DONA)

Medical Model or Technocratic Model of Childbirth

The Body is a Machine. The Body works mechanically with a rhythm like other bodies. The same time frame can be applied to all bodies.

Birth is inherently dangerous. Many things can go wrong. Women must often be rescued from the actions of her dysfunctioning body. Surgeon/doctor serves as hero/rescuer.

Tools are lab tests, results, comparison charts and objective criteria. Intuition and woman's knowledge of self/body are disregarded as unreliable and erratic.

Attendant cannot cope well with variations from statistical norm.

Attendant's desire is to "fix" things. By getting involved, s/he asserts power at the birth. After all, if the machine is not working to the normal guidelines set by other machines of this model, it must need assistance (intervention).

Baby is viewed as an additional patient needing medical skills to begin the life process. Medical caregivers often rescue the infant from injury or death. Baby is often treated as if five senses were not developed.

The medical model does not trust the process of birth or women's bodies.

Woman-Centered Model or Holistic Model of Childbirth

The Body represents the whole self of a woman—her emotional, mental, spiritual and physical selves are all reflected. The Body works to its own individual rhythm, a perfect coordination of all those influences. While it may be similar to other women's bodies, all women are individuals.

Birth is a normal function of the female body. The birthing process reflects its owner's pattern of health and living. Birth attendants ease the process through compassion and respectful, healing skills.

Objective criteria and woman's intuitive knowledge and feelings are both valid in decision making.

Variations in the birth process are expected. They require observation, evaluation and perhaps discussion.

Attendant's desire is to observe, offer support and suggestions when appropriate. Active participation is defined as charting observational information and using medical skills only when necessary. Assessment of emotional states and issues is also important.

Baby is respected as a human being with all five (six) senses intact and can begin life on his/her own, with minimal assistance, most of the time.

The woman-centered model trusts women and birth absolutely.

Both models are represented as extremes. This line illustrates the range between the two. Your viewpoint and that of your partner and medical attendant may all fall in different places on this line. The key questions to ask are:

Where are you on this continuum?
Where is your medical attendant?

Medical Model   **Holistic Model**

```
 |_____|
 |                                                        |
```

The larger the space between your viewpoints,
the greater the potential for conflict during labor and birth.

It does not matter where on the line the mother and her family are, or where the physician or midwife is. What matters is the space BETWEEN their two places on the line.

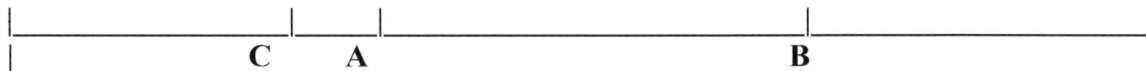

```
 |_____|___|_____|_____|
 |            C     A                      B               |
```

If a mother would place herself at line "A" and place her care provider at line "B," all the space between "A" and "B" is the potential for conflict at the birth. This graphically outlines the possibility that the mother may be dissatisfied with the care provider's decisions and recommendations at her birth.

If the mother is at line "A" but her care provider is at line "C," there is only a very small potential that the mother will be unhappy with her care.

The important thing for clients to do is to assess where they are and where their care provider is on the continuum. This will help them to feel more satisfied with the care they received after the baby is born.

References
Davis-Floyd, Robbie (1994). Birth as an American Rite of Passage. Berkeley, CA: University of California Press.
Weed, Susun (1989). Healing Wise. Ash Tree Publications.

Birth Plans (aka "Birth Preferences")

What is a Birth Plan?

The short answer is that the birth plan is a *tool to facilitate communication.* It is a written description of how you would like to be supported during labor, delivery, and immediately postpartum. It also includes your preferences for the baby during these times. Ideally, a birth plan facilitates communication on a few levels:

- Between the mother and her partner
- Between the couple and their doula and/or other members of the support team
- Between the couple and their medical care providers

A birth plan is only useful or helpful to the extent that it *facilitates* good communication, helping everyone to be on the same page.

> ### What a Birth Plan is Not
>
> ✓ A script for how your labor and birth will unfold
> ✓ A contract between you and your health care providers
> ✓ A list of procedures you want to avoid
> ✓ More than two pages of information

Planning for labor may seem overwhelming when you consider all the options that are available to you. You may wonder about the value of it, since you can't really plan how your labor will unfold and it's not realistic to plan for every possible contingency (your birth plan would be ten pages along and no one would actually read it!). Your birth plan is an introduction to you and how your support team (medical and otherwise) can best support you and your baby through this experience. It might explain what pain relief techniques you would like to try, what interventions you would like to avoid or what atmosphere you would like to cultivate in the labor room. It can help to set the tone for your birth.

Many women today are attended by doctors and midwives who work in large group practices. You may have an excellent relationship with one doctor or midwife, but there is no guarantee that she/he will be the same person who attends you in labor. And no matter how good your prenatal communication and relationship is with your doctor or midwife, you do not know the nurses at the hospital and they do not know you. A birth plan helps people get to know you at a time when you may not be in a frame of mind to introduce yourself and explain all your needs and preferences.

During labor, if situations arise in which a decision must be made, it is easy for a nurse, doula or coach to check your birth plan for guidance. It lets them know what options you would like to try and what options you would like to avoid if possible.

How to Write a Birth Plan

Understand your options.

The first step in writing a birth plan is to find out what your options are. Different doctors will give you different choices for handling the same situation. Different hospitals or birth centers will vary in environment, protocols and available options. Review the **Birth Plan Checklist** included here. Read through the list and determine what options appeal to you and what options you don't think you want. You can use this list to find out what your caregiver feels comfortable with. You should also take the Birth Plan Checklist on a hospital/birth center tour to find out how the policies may affect your options. Ask lots of questions on your tour, even if you are the only one asking questions! Some hospital tour guides may adopt an approach that is best summarized as "how to be a good patient in our hospital." When they understand that you are interested in all your options, they should be able to switch gears and accommodate you. If you are not satisfied with the options available with your current caregiver/place of birth, then you may want to explore other choices available in your area.

Examine your feelings and consider your priorities.

Once you know what choices are available to you, it is important to determine how you feel about the options. Some things will be very important and others will seem small or unimportant. There is no right or wrong; it is simply a matter of understanding who you are and how you want things handled. You may find that there are several options that you feel very strongly about. In this case, it might be helpful to use the **Ideal Birth Worksheet** (below) to work through your feelings and rank your choices according to level of importance to you. Both the mother and her partner (if any) need to decide what things are important to them and then discuss their feelings and make any necessary compromises. In the written birth plan, list your choices in order of priority, most important first.

Determine whether you can get what you want.

As you create your birth plan, be sure and bring it with you to prenatal visits with your doctor or midwife. It is important to begin this process of claiming ownership of your birth during the prenatal period and to begin a discussion with your chosen care provider. The provider can let you know if your requests are realistic, likely to be honored, or even possible within the context of your chosen birthplace and given your personal circumstances and medical history. In some cases, you may learn that your care provider does not particularly want to enter a discussion about your preferences, seems impatient with the entire subject, or flatly states that they cannot support your choices. This will help you determine if your chosen caregiver is the best match for you. If you are not getting a receptive response, consider whether there is room for negotiation and compromise. You are the customer and you are paying the bill. You have some power here, but you will only be as powerful as you believe yourself to be.

Prepare for a positive experience.
Be sure to phrase your final birth plan in a pleasant and polite tone. Do not present your preferences as a list of demands. This can help everyone feel more confident and increase your chances of having the birth experience you want.

Birth Plan Tips

✓ Make it short and easy to read.
✓ Divide it in two sections—one for labor and birth and one for postpartum mother-baby care.
✓ Put the most important items first.
✓ Use positive, flexible language (e.g., how you would like to be supported rather than what you don't want people to do).
✓ If you use a template, inject some personality into it.

Choices regarding immediate postpartum care of the newborn

Expectant parents are encouraged to consider their preferences regarding the following medical procedures and protocols commonly used with the newborn and to begin a dialogue with their care provider prior to the birth. As you sort out your priorities, you can begin to incorporate your preferences into a Birth Plan. For a hospital birth, typically it is the labor and delivery nurse's job to see that routine procedures are accomplished. If it is important to you to do some things differently than her protocols may require, then it is essential that you get her on board with your plan.

Do you have preferences about any of the following?
- Delay cord clamping until the cord has stopped pulsating.
- Refrain from routine suctioning of the baby and provide only if/when necessary.
- Allow for immediate, undisturbed, skin-to-skin contact between mom and baby.
- Stabilize baby's temperature with skin-to-skin on mom or dad rather than using warming table.
- Delay all routines until one hour postpartum (e.g., weighing, measuring, eye drops, etc.).
- Perform routine procedures bedside or even while mom is holding baby, if possible.
- Allow mom and baby time to figure out breastfeeding on their own. Provide support only if asked to do so. Care providers should ask for permission before doing any hands-on breastfeeding support techniques.
- Allow parents to be involved with giving baby his/her first bath; or have it done bedside; or delay until parents are ready.
- Rub vernix "in" rather than "off."

These procedures are routines, but may be negotiable:
- Administration of Vitamin K within first hour after birth; may need to request a waiver form
- Blood sugar checks (heel poke), especially indicated for 9+ pound babies; may request to keep baby at breast as an alternative (if baby is not breastfeeding, supplementation may be required to prevent dangerous drop in baby's blood sugar)

These procedures are required by state laws:
- Antibiotic drops in eyes within first hour after birth (prevention against possible gonorrhea infection that can result in blindness in the newborn); parents may be able to sign a waiver in some care settings.
- Newborn Screening (heel poke for blood samples); very difficult to opt out of this one; see Limitations to Parental Rights below.

These procedures require explicit parental consent (meaning you have the right to postpone or decline and they will not be done without your expressed consent):
- Circumcision
- Hepatitis B vaccine; can be delayed until 6 weeks and still compliant with American Academy of Pediatricians (AAP) recommendations.

Limitations to Parental Rights

In the United States, parents do not retain the legal right to decline recommended medical treatments for their minor children. So, once a family interfaces with the medical care system, they are at risk of losing ultimate decision-making power over their child's medical care. Of course, many doctors will include parents in treatment choices and decisions. However, if parents are refusing what doctors believe to be lifesaving treatment (e.g., antibiotics or blood transfusions), doctors can get a court order granting them legal custody of the child based on "medical neglect" on the part of the parents. These situations can become quite contentious, but the courts typically come down on the side of the medical professionals rather than the parents.

Get a Second Opinion

If treatments are being recommended for your newborn, especially treatments that require re-hospitalization of the baby or a disruption in breastfeeding (e.g., for jaundice), consider bringing in your private pediatrician for a second opinion. After all, this is the person who is going to be following your baby's care and it makes sense to involve them sooner, rather than later, if an issue is being raised by the hospital's neonatal staff.

Consider Early Discharge

If your birth went well, meaning mom feels pretty good and the baby is healthy, then you may want to consider leaving the hospital environment sooner rather than later. This will work especially well if you have a knowledgeable helper at home—perhaps your mom, a doula or an experienced friend. It is a myth that anyone "gets more rest" in the hospital and no one would ever argue that the food is good. In addition, hospitals are notorious for being a good place to acquire an infection. While you may feel a bit overwhelmed at the prospect of going it on your own, you really don't need to remain hospitalized if there are no specific health concerns.

Ideal Birth Worksheet

This exercise will help you sort out your thoughts and wishes about your upcoming birth. For this exercise, imagine you are having your perfect labor—everything works out exactly how you want it to.

The Uncontrollable Issues
In real life, you cannot control these things but if you could, how would your labor happen?
- When and where does labor begin?
- Who is with you when labor begins?
- How strong are your contractions?
- How quickly do your contractions progress?
- How long do you push?

The Almost-Controllable Issues
There are some circumstances in labor which you might have control over or might not. It all depends on how your labor unfolds. If you have a choice about these issues, how do they happen?
- How does your midwife assist you?
- Where do you labor?
- Where do you give birth?
- What tools do you use to cope with labor?
- Who labors with you?
- What techniques are used to help you?
- What techniques are not a part of your labor?
- What happens after the baby is born?

The Most Important Issues
After working through the previous two lists of questions, you should begin to have identified the issues that are most important to you. Complete these sentences.
- My top three priorities for this birth are…
- For me, the ideal place to give birth is …
- I want to be sure that the following labor tools are available at my birth …
- For my birth, the ideal clinical personnel are …
- I want to have the following people there for my emotional support and well-being …
- For me, the best approach to pain relief is …
- The following are also very important to me …

Birth Plan Checklist

Use this checklist to make sure you have covered everything you feel is important in your birth plan. You do not need to have something written for all these areas; this is only a list of areas you *may* have strong preferences about.

- Important Issues
  - Concerns (Why? Tell your story, briefly)
  - Health Issues
  - Fears
- Pain Management Preferences
  - 1st stage medications
  - Epidural
  - Water immersion
  - Non-drug comfort measures
  - Consider requesting that staff refrain from offering pain meds or asking you to rate your pain if you are attempting a natural birth
- Medical interventions you wish to use or avoid
  - For inducing or speeding up labor
  - For pain management
  - For monitoring
  - Routine administration of Pitocin for third stage (a.k.a. "active management")
- 2nd Stage
  - Positions you are willing/wishing to try
  - Style of pushing
  - Preferences for perineal support
- Preferences in case of cesarean
  - Type of cut on uterus (low transverse vs. vertical)
  - Who should remain with mother/baby?
  - Skin-to-skin with baby as soon as possible
- Postpartum care of baby
  - Immediate undisturbed skin-to-skin with baby?
  - Delay cutting the cord until it stops pulsing?
  - Timing of routine assessments (e.g., weighing, measuring, newborn exam, etc.)
  - Routine medical interventions (e.g., Vitamin K, eye prophylaxis)?
  - Breastfeeding?
  - Rooming in or baby to nursery?
  - First bath
  - Intact penis or circumcision?
  - Consent to Hepatitis B vaccine or no?
- Other Important Items
  - Identification of support team
  - Photos/videos
  - Privacy needs
  - Environmental issues (lighting, music)

      o   When to discharge
      o   Educational needs (anything you want to be sure to learn about baby care before you leave)

Sources

Written by Patty Brennan; partially adapted from the following.

- Jennifer Vanderlaan, http://www.birthingnaturally.net/birthplan/what.html. Check out this helpful site for a variety of birth plan templates, sample birth plans, and related resources.
- http://www.childbirth.org/interactive/ibirthplan.html
- http://www.fensende.com/~swnymph/birthplan.all.html

Talking to Health Care Providers
By Kim James, BDT(DONA)

Aim to be collaborative partners. Both you and your health care provider want what is best for you. Be confident about what you want. Share what you know and ask your care provider to fill in the blanks and provide the background for their suggestions. Don't be afraid to point out when your knowledge differs from their suggestions and recommendations.

1. Explain what you want:
   I am hoping that it's possible to …
   Is there any reason we cannot …?
   What would it take for me to be able to …?

2. Explain why you want it:
   I lean toward _____ treatments and believe _____
   I am hoping to achieve _____ because of _____
   I strongly value _____ because my background is _____
   I'm most comfortable making decisions when _____
   My best sources of information come from _____

3. Listen carefully to your health care provider's recommendations:
   Active listening with an open mind and heart allows you to see the reason and reasoning behind your care provider's suggestions. It also sets the expectation for the kind of listening you expect in return.

4. Clarify for understanding:
   Could you tell me more about this? (Make sure you understand what the concern is.)
   Is this a routine recommendation or is this a specific recommendation for me and my situation?
   Are there other things I can do? (Is this the only solution or are there other choices?)
   What happens if I wait? (Lets you know how quickly you must decide.)
   What are the risks of doing nothing? (Helps determine how serious the problem is.)
   What is the likelihood of that happening?

5. Make a decision.

Always use your BRAIN
Benefits
Risks
Alternatives
Intuition
Nothing

Informed Decision Making:
Choosing Medical Interventions

Yes	**Maybe**	**No**
Use medical tools when the benefits of the tool clearly outweigh the harms.	Ask more questions when the benefits and risks are similar or unclear. If mother and baby are okay now, consider waiting a little longer before acting.	Do not use elective, routine or purely convenient medical interventions which can result in HIGHER complication rates for mother and baby.

Find out what is going on.
- What is the problem?
- Could you tell me more about this?
- What are my treatment options?

Assess your risk.
- Are my personal odds higher or lower than the average? You may have health or demographic factors that affect your relative risk for undesirable obstetrical outcomes.
- Is this a routine recommendation or is this a specific recommendation for me and my situation?
- What factors increase my likelihood of having this happen?
- Why are you recommending this for me?

Assess alternative treatments.
- Are there other things I can do?
- What are my treatment options?
- What happens if I wait?

Consider waiting.
- What happens if we watch and wait?
- Is there a chance we are over-treating by acting now?
- Are we treating a known problem or are we treating a potential for a problem?

Birth Plan Guidelines
By Amy Gilliland, Ph.D., BDT(DONA)

1. Start out with a general statement introducing yourself, your philosophy and possibly your reasons for choosing this hospital or birth center.

2. Use positive language whenever possible.

3. In general, it is more positive and descriptive to state what you do want rather than what you don't want. "To avoid an episiotomy or tearing of the perineal tissues, please use warm compresses and help me to breathe the baby out slowly."

4. Be specific. "I want to be free to move around during labor as I choose," rather than "I want an active birth."

5. Don't try to cover everything, only those areas most important to you. The reader can get bogged down in detail and your main message can be lost.

6. Use organizational headings that help to guide the reader. Some suggestions are" During Labor—First Stage; Birth; Infant Care; Supporting Breastfeeding; Emergencies. You may or may not want to title the introductory paragraph.

7. Some parents wish to include sections on emergencies such as a cesarean operation, intensive care for their infant or the baby's death.

8. As you read what you have written, ask yourself: "How do I feel reading this?" Put yourself in the place of a birth parent, hospital staff member and doctor.

9. Ask your caregiver to confirm your discussions and approach by signing the document. You may also wish to sign along with your partner and doula.

10. If you are planning a homebirth it is wise to prepare both a homebirth plan and a hospital birth plan. It is especially important if you will be arriving at the hospital after a complication at home. In some areas it is unwise to reveal your homebirth arrangements. You may wish to discuss this further with your midwife or doctor.

11. When completed, use a highlighter pen to call attention to the most important phrases (like the use of bold type on this sheet of guidelines).

Pain Medication Preference Scale

+10	She wants to feel nothing; desires anesthesia before labor begins.
+9	Fear of pain; lack of confidence that she will be able to cope; dependence on staff for pain relief.
+7	Definite desire for anesthesia as soon in labor as the doctor will allow it, or before labor becomes painful.
+5	Desire for epidural anesthesia in active labor (4-5 cm); willingness to cope until then, perhaps with narcotic medications.
+3	Desire to use some pain medication but wants as little as possible; plans to use self-help comfort measures for part of labor.
0	No opinion or preference. This is a rare attitude among pregnant women, but not uncommon among partners or support people.
-3	Prefers that pain medication be avoided but wants medication as soon as she requests it in labor.
-5	Strong preference to avoid pain medications, mainly for benefit to baby and labor progress.
-7	Very strong desire for natural childbirth, for sense of personal gratification as well as to benefit baby and labor progress. Will be disappointed if she uses medications.
-9	Wants medication to be denied by staff, even if she asks for it.
-10	Wants no medication, even for cesarean delivery.

What is Support?

Support is unconditional.

It is listening …
not judging, not telling your own story
.

Support is not offering advice …
it is offering a tissue, a touch, a hug … caring.

We are here to help a woman discover what she is feeling …
not to make the feelings go away.

We are here to help a woman identify her options …
not to tell her which options to choose.

We are here to discuss steps with a woman …
not to take the steps for her.

We are here to help a woman discover her own strength …
not to rescue her and leave her still vulnerable.

We are here to help a woman discover she can help herself …
not to take that responsibility for her.

We are here to help a woman learn to choose …
not to make it unnecessary for her to make difficult choices.

Scope of Practice
Small Group Exercise

A. Self-Determination/Client Empowerment
1. Discuss the difference between "advice" and "information."
2. What can doulas do or say in place of saying, "I think you should …"?
3. How do you respond if the client says, "What would you do if you were me?"
4. Brainstorm empowerment strategies/skills doulas can use with clients to help them become their own best advocates.

B. Client Confidentiality
1. List information, in addition to their name, that might identify someone.
2. What precautions should doulas take online to protect client confidentiality?
3. What are some safe ways to seek support from sister doulas (e.g., process a challenging birth, problem-solve a client issue, or identify needed resources) without violating client confidentiality?

C. Professionalism and Trustworthiness
1. List both valid and lame reasons why a doula might miss a birth or be unavailable to complete services to a client.
2. Discuss how you might integrate a back-up doula (or two) into your doula practice.
3. Under what circumstances should you activate your back-up doula?
4. How much of the birth fee do you think is fair to pay your back-up doula?

D. Refund Policies for Doulas
Birth doulas generally charge one fee for a package of services that includes prenatal visits, on-call labor and birth support, and a minimum of one postpartum visit. I recommend that the doula collect half her fee when first hired as a "non-refundable" deposit to save space in her schedule, with the balance due at the last prenatal visit (before the "on-call" period starts).

1. Under what circumstances should a doula refund the client's fee or a portion of the fee?
2. What about a missed birth?
3. What if the client hired the doula to help her achieve a VBAC and she ended up with a cesarean?

Volunteer Opportunities for Doulas
Complete certification requirements.

Southeastern Michigan

Southeast Michigan Doula Project
Community-based nonprofit that connects low-income pregnant women and teens with volunteer birth and postpartum doulas.
www.MIdoula.org
southeastmidoulas@gmail.com
586-834-8748

Dial-a-Doula
- Program that pairs women going into labor at the University of Michigan Hospital with trained volunteer birth doulas.
- Volunteers sign up to be on-call for 12-hour shifts based on their availability
- Email dialadoula@umich.edu

Abigayle Ministries
Abigayle Ministries is a Christian interdenominational non-profit organization in Sterling Heights, MI. The ministry assists adult pregnant women and their children by introducing them to the Gospel of Jesus Christ and equipping them to be self-sufficient through its residential housing program. Doula support is needed for residents in the program.
https://www.abigayleministries.org/
abigayles@abigayleministries.org (Put Doula Volunteer in subject line)
586-323-1411

Facebook: Join Metro Detroit Doulas and Childbirth Educators Group

West Michigan

MomsBloom (Postpartum Support Services)
Located in Kent County, this non-profit that offers hands-on and emotional peer support and advocacy to women as they navigate the challenges of early motherhood. Volunteers are trained to provide weekly support to any Kent County family with a newborn, free of charge. Whether mom needs help with preparing a meal, rocking a baby or reading a story to a sibling so that mom can shower and rest, no task is too small. If you'd like to join the MomSquad, please reach us at katie@momsbloom.org or call 616-828-1021.

Facebook: Join Michigan Doulas Group

The Birth Marathon:
Food and Drink for Labor and Birth

By Patty Brennan, excerpted from
Whole Family Recipes: For the Childbearing Year and Beyond

Despite research that concludes that moms should have access to food and drink in labor, many moms birthing in U.S. hospitals today are faced with instructions to not eat solid food and are restricted to ingesting clear liquids only. If labor goes on longer than your blood sugar can hold out and contractions or your energy begin to wane, try the following options. Your overall strategy here is to achieve a stable blood sugar throughout labor. This can be challenging, not just due to restrictive hospital policies and the limitations of what is available on site, but because:

- some women feel nauseous from the onset of labor
- some women respond to pain with nausea and vomiting
- digestion does slow considerably during active labor because blood flow is concentrated to the uterus
- you may not have an appetite
- you may fear vomiting (remember, however, that nausea is one of the symptoms caused by low blood sugar!)

Strategies

- Some women experience an urge to load up on carbohydrates in the 24-hour period before the onset of active labor, like what an athlete may do in preparation for running a marathon on the following day. Go for it! (I had a bread, salad and pasta dinner at a local restaurant 12 hours before my second child was born and never felt nauseated in labor, which started about 5 hours after the meal.) This strategy is especially recommended if you are facing a scheduled induction. You don't want the hard work to hit after you've been essentially fasting for 24 hours or more.

- EAT WHILE YOU ARE STILL AT HOME IN EARLY LABOR. This is key and must be maintained throughout the day. Don't just settle for breakfast and stop there. Eat every 2–3 hours, whatever appeals. You may want to avoid heavy, greasy foods such as pizza or fast foods (which don't digest easily under the best of circumstances).

- Avoid substances that will spike your blood sugar such as pop and other forms of concentrated sugar (read your labels!). These will dehydrate you and ultimately lead to your blood sugar crashing.

- Eat a banana on the way to the birth center/hospital. Despite most TV depictions of how women go into labor (i.e., a sudden contraction alerts her to the need to rush to the hospital where she gives birth soon after on her back, typically involving various emergencies for dramatic effect), most women have plenty of time to take care of themselves at home and head to the birthing center/hospital with little need for high drama.

- During labor, try a variety of the suggestions below, alternating them. A little protein here, some electrolytes there, something sweet to boost your energy, the Pregnancy Tea … you get the idea. That will keep you going if your labor is long. This is especially important for women who might be admitted to the hospital early in labor or whose labor is being induced.

- Drink lots of water, at least 4 ounces per hour throughout your labor, more if it's a hot day and you're sweating a lot. Have your support team help you with this. (Note to partners and doulas: It's your job to encourage the mom to drink throughout her labor. If she is willing to drink, asking for it and consistently taking several gulps when offered, then just keep the supply coming and keep an eye on her to ensure she doesn't stop drinking at some point. However, if the mom is disinterested in drinking and reluctant to do so, then frequent small sips will be necessary. Keep offering!)

- Finally, don't hesitate to accept IV fluids if you can't keep anything down over a long period of time and are getting dehydrated. While most healthy women will not need routine IV fluids, dehydration can cause your labor to be dysfunctional and nonproductive. An IV can turn the picture around and is an appropriate use of medical intervention.

Raspberry Leaf Tea Labor Cubes
Before labor begins, make up a VERY strong tea (two quarts of boiling water with 2 cups of dried red raspberry leaves added). Simmer with the lid off for at least 20–30 minutes as the volume reduces considerably. Strain and add ¼ cup of honey (raw is best if possible). Pour into ice cube trays and freeze, adding water, if necessary, for at least one tray's worth. Store in a zippy bag at home or take with you to the birth center/hospital (usually you can store them in the freezer of the small room refrigerator or in the common "nutrition room" refrigerator). The honey gives mom a boost of energy, while the concentrated raspberry leaves provide minerals and may assist in bringing back strong contractions. In between the contractions, mom can easily crunch the cubes into a satisfying slush.

Electrolyte-Balanced Sports Drinks
There are a large variety of sports drinks on the market these days. Avoid the overly sweet, chemically generated metallic blue and other colored products not found in nature. See what's available at your local health food store and find something you like. Have 2–3 quarts on hand for labor (your support team will appreciate these as well). I like a product called Recharge and it comes in several flavors.

Miso Broth
If you're unfamiliar, miso is a paste made from fermented soybeans. It is high in protein and tastes salty. If you haven't tried miso, there are several different flavors available in the refrigerated section of your local health food store. Give them a try and find one you like. The paste can be brought with you to the hospital and kept in the refrigerator. Mix one tablespoon of miso into one cup of hot water. Avoid boiling miso as it kills many of the nutrients. There are also packets of instant "miso soup" on the market. This is a good option for doulas and midwives to carry with their birth supplies.

Concentrated Home-Made Chicken or Beef Broth
Place one whole (preferably organic) chicken or a couple of beef bones in a large soup pot. Bring to a boil and spoon off the scum that will rise to the surface over a 10-minute period and discard. Roughly cut up 1 onion, 3 carrots (washed, with skins on) and 3 stalks of celery, including tops. Chop up 2–3 garlic cloves and throw those in too (you can even leave the skins on as a timesaver). Cover and reduce heat, simmering for 1½ hours. Allow cooling and strain out the solids (make chicken salad with the meat). Put in refrigerator overnight so that the layer of fat on top solidifies. In the morning, remove and discard the fat layer, but don't worry if a little is left behind. Return the broth to the stove uncovered and bring to a boil, allowing the liquid to reduce to a rich-colored (and tasty!) broth. Add in salt to taste at the very end. Freeze in small containers to have on hand for labor.

Herb Tea and Honey
Bring a variety of your favorite herbal teabags and some raw honey with you to the hospital. When energy flags, especially in the second stage of labor, a cup of tea with a generous spoonful of honey can give you the boost you need to get the job done. Ginger tea can settle the stomach if nausea is an issue.

Hot Drinks
Americans are big on iced drinks, but in many parts of the world, ingesting iced drinks is not recommended. Many cultures, from China to South America, have prohibitions against iced drinks for women in labor or postpartum. The wise women grandmas-to-be will not allow it. Feed the fire. You are supposed to get hot in labor! You will sweat. You will be uncomfortable. It's okay. It's more efficient.

Labor Food
Women have been using tubes of concentrated carbohydrates found in the runners' stores (aka "goo"). Lots of flavors, promoted as digesting rapidly and easily while vigorously exercising, and easy to just take a squirt. Be sure and follow up with water as it is very concentrated. Rave reviews from birthing moms.

Other Labor Foods
- bananas (worth mentioning twice due to portability and high potassium content)
- yogurt or kefir or fruit smoothies
- light foods that appeal

Cheat Sheet for the Birth Partner

Early Labor (at home)

- Encourage mom to eat to appetite
- Remind her to drink fluids.
- Help her to REST for the big event (no last-minute housecleaning!).
- Remind mom to keep her bladder empty.
- If labor starts in the middle of the night, encourage mom to go back to sleep.
- Keep mom company and distract her—walk with her, play cards, watch TV, dance, etc.
- Encourage mom to change positions frequently, favoring upright positions.
- Time contractions, from time to time, and keep a written record. (Time from onset of one contraction to the onset of the next one; that is the frequency of the contractions. Also note how long the contraction lasts.) Do this for an hour or so and then put the stopwatch aside. Can check again later if it feels like things are picking up.
- Watch mom for visible signs of tension, especially in response to contractions, and help her to relax (baths, massage, deep breathing, verbal reminders).
- If mom seems anxious, ask her what she needs to feel safe.
- Ask her if there is anything she needs done around the house "to feel ready."
- Keep your care providers and support team updated.
- Realize that if you tell friends and family that you are in labor, you are inviting their energy and possible intrusion into the experience. Would it be better to let them know after the baby is born?
- Protect her from any negative people or influences.
- Tell her how well she is doing.
- Enjoy this time together.

> *Eat, Drink, Pee, Rest, Sleep, Distraction, Encouragement, Relax, Protect, Emotional Support*

Active Labor

- Eliminate distractions in the environment; add to comfort with pillows, dimmed lights, music, etc.
- Control the presence of visitors, in alignment with your birth plan.
- Help navigate any decisions regarding her care, using your birth plan as a guide.
- Keep lips and mouth moist.
- Give her a back massage.
- Encourage her to drink fluids and urinate at least once per hour.
- Encourage mom to change positions frequently, favoring upright positions.
- Remember the 3 R's—Rhythm, Relaxation, Ritual.
- Recognize when she is coping well (rhythmic movement, relaxation) and protect the ritual.

- Help her find a ritual that works if she is struggling.
- Suggest immersion in water (if she is able) or a shower.
- Tell her you are proud of her.

Drink, Pee, Protect, Informed Decision Making, the 3 R's,
Massage, Support, Move, Encourage, Guide, Praise

Transition

- Remind her to take one contraction at a time.
- Breathe with her.
- Help her to rest and relax between contractions (big breath out).
- If she panics, move in close, establish eye contact and help her stay focused for every contraction.
- Change the ritual if the one she was using isn't working any more.
- Expect it to get a little hairy; this just means that she is progressing (remind her of this!).
- Remember that this is usually the shortest part of labor.
- Don't give up on her if she gives up on herself.
- Hold intent for her if she has lost it temporarily.
- Validate her feelings.
- Tell her that you love her.

Face-to-Face, Breathe, Stay Calm, Hold Intent, Validate, Reassure

---

2nd Stage/Descent and Birth of Baby

- Help her find the most comfortable and productive position
- Whisper words of encouragement. "You're doing just fine." "Just like that."
- Encourage her to rest between contractions.
- Remind care providers about any key items in the birth plan related to 2nd stage and immediate postpartum care for the baby (e.g., hot compresses to perineum, skin-to-skin, delayed cord clamping, etc.).
- Enjoy your baby!

Positioning Support, Encouragement, Advocacy, Delight

3rd Stage/Delivery of Placenta

- Stay focused on the mom and the birth (it's not over yet; phone calls can wait).
- If she is reluctant, remind her that there are no bones in the placenta ("Almost done.").

- Give her a drink of something sweet.
- If she is shaky, ask the nurse to get her warm blankets.
- Encourage skin-to-skin contact with the baby.
- Continue to advocate for birth plan, as needed.
- Enjoy your baby!

Focus, Drinks, Warmth, Protect, Celebrate

Immediate Postpartum Recovery (First Two Hours)
- Keep mom and baby together, skin-to-skin.
- Baby will likely want to latch at the breast if given access. Ask for privacy if you like.
- Now you can make your calls! (Make an assessment whether you want visitors right away.)
- Take pictures.
- Have a meal.
- Celebrate!
- REST.

Skin-to-Skin, Breastfeeding, Privacy, Eat, Pictures, Celebrate, Rest

If Things Don't Go as Planned
- Help with informed decision making. Remember the questions:
    1. How will this help mom or baby?
    2. Can you describe the procedure involved?
    3. What are the risks or unintended consequences?
    4. Urgency? What are the consequences of giving it more time?
    5. Choices? Is there anything else that can be tried instead?
- Continue to advocate for pieces of the Birth Plan that can still be accomplished (e.g., skin-to-skin immediately after a cesarean delivery may be possible, even while mom is still on the operating table).
- Try to minimize the downside of any medical interventions (e.g., she does not need to lie flat on her back in bed just because she has fetal monitors strapped on or even an epidural in place).
- Understand that you are doing your best and that birth is unpredictable. Hang in there.

Informed Consent, Advocacy, Adaptation, Stay with It

Additional Suggestions for Partners & Doulas

- Wear comfortable clothing and shoes. You could be on your feet for a long time.
- Bring a bathing suit or pair of shorts that you can wear in the shower (or birth tub, if that is part of your plan).
- Bring a change of clothes.
- Pack food and drink for yourself.
- Keep your breath fresh by bringing a toothbrush and toothpaste.
- Bring a copy of the birth plan and have a good understanding of mom's wishes and desires.
- Recruit additional help for the labor room if you are feeling like you could use some support.

BRING: Comfortable Clothing, Food and Drink, Breath Freshener, Birth Plan

Positions for Labor

Squatting Positions
- Squat with rebozo and partner; doula wears rebozo around her hips while mom hangs on and squats
- Rebozo suspended over closed door; mom straddles large peanut ball
- Lap squat: mom straddles partner's lap, facing him/her; partner grasps own wrists behind mom to secure her; doula behind mom for safety – OR –
- Lap squat with doula behind partner AND rebozo for safety
- Lap squat reverse position, mom leans back on partner
- Dangle (partner sits on ledge, each foot on a stool; mom places arms over partner's upper legs and dangles)

Standing Positions
- Forward leaning/swaying
- Forward leaning/swaying w/ball on table
- Slow dancing w/partner (mom sets the rhythm, partner follows)
- Add figure-8 to slow dance w/partner

Sitting Positions
- On ball (rocking, figure-8, light bouncing)
- Backwards-facing chair (toilet), resting forward
- Two-partner pass on birth ball; mom on ball, leans back on partner; doula in front; moms is passive as her two helpers pass her back and forth
- Forward leaning into partner on ball; mom on ball, partner on chair, mom leans into partner; doula has access to her back
- Semi-lunge in bed with peanut ball (2 variations)
- Rebozo pull to release pelvis (2nd stage); rebozo around doula's waste; mom in sitting position, pulls on rebozo while bearing down

Kneeling Positions
- Kneeling – leaning in
- Over ball – add swaying
- Over top of birth bed
- Forward leaning over peanut ball
- Fire hydrant with peanut ball

Lying Down Positions
- Side-lying with pillows/bolster
- Tuck with peanut ball

Breastfeeding Primer

By Barbara Robertson, MA, IBCLC
The Breastfeeding Center of Ann Arbor, www.bfcaa.com

Benefits of Breastfeeding
- Breast milk was designed to feed human babies. It is the perfect food for your baby.
- Antibodies in breast milk protect the baby from illness; lower incidence of ear infections, colic and gastro-intestinal illness.
- Breastfeeding is associated with a lower incidence of sudden infant death syndrome (SIDS).
- Breastfed babies have a decreased likelihood for allergies, dental caries and obesity.
- Breastfeeding promotes appropriate jaw, teeth and speech development, as well as overall facial development.
- Breastfeeding promotes attachment and bonding between mother and baby.
- Breastfeeding improves IQ scores in children.
- Breastfeeding helps the mother to recover from birth.
    - Promotes normal contraction and involution of the uterus, helping it to return to its pre-pregnancy size and position in the pelvis
    - Aids in postpartum weight loss
    - Contributes to normal hormonal increases and decreases associated with post-birth emotional and physical health.
- Breast milk offers your baby less exposure to corn derivatives used in the production of formula and allows you to have control over the food that goes into making your baby's milk.
- Breast milk offers your baby less exposure to pesticides, bovine growth hormone and antibiotics inherent in non-organic, commercially produced milk used to make formula.
- Soy-based formulas can act as hormone mimics and interfere with normal hormone levels and actions in the body, affecting proper sex-differentiated development (see article at www.mothering.com, "Whole Soy Story: The Dark Side of America's Favorite Health Food" (Kaayla T. Daniel, *Mothering Magazine* Issue 124: May/June 2004).

Comfortable Nursing
- Set up a nursing station:
    - Make a couple of comfortable places in your house to nurse, one that is private, one that is more in the center of things.
    - Ideally it would be a comfy chair that rocks, but any comfy chair, couch or bed will work.
    - Table nearby, within easy reach
    - Foot stool to prop up feet if needed

- - Try to just lay back, scoot your bottom out, tuck your tail bone under, and get comfy yourself. During feeds try and have baby's body rest on your body (see Biological Nurturing website [www.BiologicalNuturing.com] for more information.
- Make sure water and a snack are available while breastfeeding.
- Entertain yourself:
  - You'll spend a lot of time nursing in the first weeks, so make it enjoyable.
  - Develop an easy nursing activity that you love and look forward to.
  - Watch TV, read, listen to radio programs or music on an iPod …
  - Make a place for your laptop on a nearby table and perfect your one-handed typing.
  - Engage in any activity that helps you lose yourself and keep from watching the clock.
- Nursing to sleep at night:
  - Get comfy! The side lying or laid-back positions are often best when you are tired.
  - Set up a low light near the place that you will nurse to sleep at night so that you can read.
  - Use your iPod with headphones while nursing to sleep.

How often and how long should I nurse?

- Women are often surprised to discover that it is normal for an exclusively breastfed infant to nurse every 1½ hours in the first couple of weeks. Feeding may last 30 minutes to one hour. Frequent feeding promotes adequate weight gain. Furthermore, milk production follows the principle of "supply and demand." Nursing at least 8–15 times every 24 hours will assure a sufficient milk supply to meet the baby's needs.
- Remember: Feedings are variable in duration and intensity during the early weeks. The ZEN of breastfeeding is to "watch the baby, not the clock." Check for adequate wets and stools. It is the frequency of breastfeeding rather than the duration that stimulates milk production.

Is my baby getting enough?

- New mothers are typically concerned about whether their milk supply is sufficient. You will know if the baby is getting enough calories by counting daily stools and wet diapers. Within the first 24–48 hours the baby will pass his first stool, called meconium, which is dark and tarry. By days three to six, the baby should have two to five yellow seedy stools in a 24-hour period.
- During the first two to four days, babies wet only a couple times per day. By day five or six, as mother's milk becomes more plentiful, a baby should have six to eight wet diapers in a 24-hour period. Urine should be relatively odorless and clear to pale yellow in color.
- Signs of dehydration in infants include:
  - Lethargy
  - Sunken soft spot (anterior fontanel) on the baby's skull
  - Dry, loose skin

- Diminished or absent wet diapers with concentrated urine or orange staining due to uric acid crystals
- Dry mucous membranes (look in the baby's mouth—are saliva bubbles visible?)
- Temperature; and fast respirations (persistently greater than 30–50 breaths per minute). (These last two symptoms may also indicate infection in the newborn, which is an emergency.)

Weight Gain

- Initially babies typically lose up to 10 percent of their birth weight. By day three to five, the baby will begin gaining about ½ to 1 ounce per day. Babies should regain their birth weight by day 10. After day 10, babies should be gaining a minimum of 4 ounces per week. If infants follow this pattern, you can feel confident that they are getting enough milk.
- Be aware that weighing the baby on different scales (such as one at the hospital, one at home, and one at the pediatrician's office) is likely to yield slight differences in calibration which do not reflect a failure-to-thrive or insufficient milk supply problem. Weighing the baby too frequently (daily or more than once per day) should be discouraged. Trust your eyes and intuition as well.

Inadequate Milk Supply

- Be confident in your ability to produce enough milk (most moms can) but watch for signs of inadequate intake:
  - Not enough wet diapers (less than 6–8 per day)
  - Not enough poopy diapers (less than 4 quarters worth per day)
  - Not gaining weight well (a minimum of 4 oz. per week after birth weight has been re-gained by day 10 or so)
  - Baby is often fussy or dissatisfied on the breast or right after a feeding.

Engorged/Sore Breasts

- If associated with the milk "coming in," not to worry, this will resolve on its own shortly; give the baby frequent access; if super uncomfortable, try pumping a bit off to soften your breasts to a more tolerable level; your body will automatically regulate the milk supply.
- Fresh green cabbage leaves, when applied directly to the breasts as a compress, also help to relieve discomfort. Once the leaves have wilted, replace with fresh leaves until relieved.
- Try eating a lot of watermelon and cucumbers. Both are diuretics and will help your body clear excess fluids. Moms who received IV fluids over a period of many hours during labor may have lots of edema, especially noticeable in the ankles and face, but also adding to the swollen breast tissue. The solution is simple and delicious.
- Could indicate a change in nursing frequency
- May be normal change in baby's nutritional needs
- May indicate a problem (watch for other signs of illness or concerning changes in baby)

- May be a plugged duct or the first sign of mastitis
- Go right to bed with the baby
- Extra nursing
- Lots of rest
- Drink extra water
- Massage breasts, especially while nursing
- Place a warm compress on sore area of breast
- Take warm showers or baths
- Avoid taking antibiotics unless full blown mastitis develops and does not improve with rest/nursing/hydration (could lead to thrush)

Cracked or Sore Nipples
- Baby is most likely having trouble with latch.
- Get some help!

Early intervention is key when experiencing nursing trouble.
- Call your local La Leche League leader/group.
- Hire a lactation consultant, preferably one with the credentials IBCLC (International Board-Certified Lactation Consultant).
- Work with a breastfeeding-friendly physician.

Postpartum Planning Guide

These are guidelines for the first few weeks following an uneventful birth. In the case of twins, prolonged or difficult labor and birth, cesarean delivery, maternal hemorrhage, severe perineal lacerations, or health issues with the baby requiring extended hospitalization, your plan should allow extra time for care and recovery.

Plan for household help. Recruit the support of one or two mentally positive people to free the mother of household responsibilities (laundry, shopping, errands, cleaning, meal preparation, childcare for older siblings) for two to six weeks. Your support folks should be able to see what needs doing and do it without lots of direction. There is to be no guilt involved with asking for help! If extended family support is available to you, that can work or, if you can afford it, consider hiring a postpartum doula. To learn more about the role of postpartum doulas, see the article "All about Doulas: A Consumers' Guide to Getting the Help You Need" at www.center4cby.com.

Control visitors. Inform close friends and family when you are ready for visitors after birth. It is important to control who, when, how many at a time, and for how long you want to welcome visitors. You will, no doubt, be eager to show off your baby. On the other hand, visitors arriving just as you have an opportunity to sleep, or when you should be focusing on breastfeeding your baby, will likely prove to be more stressful than enjoyable. Turn the ringer off your phone to sleep. Post signs saying "We are sleeping now. Please come another time." Plan for short visits and ask guests to bring food or help with chores. Remember that people who have never had a baby before will be relatively clueless as to your needs. You will need to clue them in. Failure to control the number and timing of visitors is probably the most common mistake new parents make.

Sleep when the baby sleeps. Calculate the average amount of sleep you need to feel okay under normal circumstances. Can you normally get by with six or seven hours, or do you need eight or nine to feel well? You will still need this same amount of sleep after the baby is born, though admittedly it will be interrupted sleep. One strategy is to not get up and get dressed, receive visitors, or go about your day until you have managed to sleep your required amount. On some days, this may be well into the afternoon hours. Resist the temptation to "do everything" when the baby is sleeping if you have not gotten your eight hours (or whatever) in during the last twenty-four hours. The more you rest now, the sooner you will recover.

Heal. Listen to your body and take care of yourself. Milk supply and postpartum healing are your top priorities. In addition to sleeping, make sure you are drinking plenty of fluids and eating properly. Take sitz baths if you have stitches—even two or three times per day to promote healing and control pain. Remember healing is a *process* rather than a *result*. And healing takes time.

Recruit help with meals. Make a list of things your family likes to eat. Post this list on the refrigerator for all to see. This provides a quick answer for those asking to bring a meal. It may be helpful to appoint someone to organize meals for the family. Online calendars are a great tool. When folks sign up to drop off a meal, make it easy for a meal to be left for you without necessarily having to be awake to receive the meal or invite guests in (e.g., a cooler on the porch). In addition, you may want to freeze some meals ahead of time and stock up on non-perishables. Use these when your helpers start to fade.

Consider paying for help. This may include housecleaning, childcare for your other children, using a diaper service for the first six weeks, or hiring a postpartum doula. If you can't afford to hire help, perhaps ask for help as a shower gift rather than accumulating a bunch of stuff that you don't really need.

Ask for what you need. Postpartum can be emotionally high and low all at the same time. Hormones are changing dramatically. You may just need someone to listen to you and validate your feelings about your birth, about becoming a mother, or other challenges you are experiencing. Lots of new parents are disturbed by some of the emotions they are experiencing postpartum as they go through this tremendous adjustment to parenthood. It's okay. Talk about it. You are not alone.

Have realistic expectations. Newborns "only" sleep, eat and poop, but they do it every hour (or so). It takes more time and energy than most people realize. Imagine a sphere about 1" in diameter. That's how big a newborn's tummy is! As breast milk is easily digested, it moves quickly out of the stomach and the baby is hungry again. As your baby grows, he/she will grow a bigger stomach and be able to space out their feedings a bit more. Each one is different, some sleeping five hours at a stretch from the early weeks on, and others waking every hour and a half to nurse for months. Let your baby lead the way at first. Try and keep it in perspective; things change quickly.

Understand that siblings go through adjustment too. While accepting help to care for them, try to keep established rituals intact so that your child doesn't feel abandoned or utterly displaced. If you normally read a book to your child before bedtime, then make every effort to continue to do so. It is not uncommon for toddlers to relapse with toilet training efforts when there is a new baby in the house (don't despair with this!). Consider recruiting helpers to take your child for an outing. Breastfeeding mothers of toddlers find that having a "special" basket of toys that only comes out when it's time to nurse the baby is a good strategy. Or limit video watching to only breastfeeding times, or listen to books on CD together, to be continued at the next breastfeeding session…. You can get creative here.

Take a little time for yourself each day. At first, it can feel as though, if you are meeting the baby's needs, then your needs don't get met. It is only normal that you may feel sad or even resentful about this. Try to identify what activity you miss the most. Are you longing for a walk in fresh air, girlfriend time, computer play time, or missing your exercise regime? Try to carve out even a half hour where you and your partner give each other permission to get at least that one need met. Make a list right now of three things you find relaxing, rejuvenating or inspiring.

Don't forget to take time for each other. Many new moms experience a drop in their sex drive for a while after giving birth. This is normal, it's okay, and it will return. Breastfeeding a baby involves a great deal of intimacy and new moms may feel "touched out." A fear that sex will hurt, especially if there was trauma to the perineum or vagina, is understandable. Also, your hormones are not helping because your body is not really trying to get pregnant right now. With the ebb and flow of cycles and desire, you may find yourself solidly in the ebb for a while. For breastfeeding mothers, the hormones that promote fertility and the presence of cervical mucus remain suppressed (timing is variable on this, lasting anywhere from a few weeks postpartum through the full time that mom breastfeeds). This means that the vagina may be dryer than usual, requiring lubrication for sex to feel comfortable. There are all kinds of intimacy. A dinner by candlelight, a "date night," a walk together without the baby, or willingness to pleasure your partner without feeling you must respond in kind are all creative solutions. Patience and mutual consideration are key.

Postpone major life changes. When possible, avoid moving or changing jobs during the childbearing year (pregnancy through at least three months postpartum). Many new parents imagine they require more space for their expanding family. Maybe you don't need a nursery or a bigger home or all that baby gear. Keep it simple and play it by ear. Having a baby is change enough.

Develop a support network. Hook up with both new and experienced parents for support, guidance and feedback. In the end, this will normalize what you are experiencing OR perhaps help you determine that your situation is not normal and that you need extra help. Either way, it should prove validating.

Give yourself credit. Parenting is a huge life change, bringing more love and laughter into your life along with new challenges. The difficult times and the adoration you feel for your baby do not necessarily balance out to a happy medium. It can be both joyful and hard. It may take some time for you to find your new rhythm.

Additional Resources

Books

- Brennan, Patty. *Ready for Birth and Baby Workbook;* childbirth preparation class manual; www.LifespanDoulas.com.
- Brennan, Patty. *The Doula Business Guide: How to Succeed as a Birth, Postpartum or End-of-Life Doula,* 3rd Edition (2019); www.LifespanDoulas.com.
- Brennan, Patty. *The Doula Business Guide Workbook: Tools to Create a Thriving Practice,* 3rd Edition (2019); www.LifespanDoulas.com.
- England and Horowitz. *Birthing from Within;* use of birth art to process fears and emotions as preparation for birth.
- Noble, Elizabeth. *Essential Exercises for the Childbearing Year*; includes a full chapter on the pelvic floor.
- Romm, Aviva Jill. *The Natural Pregnancy Book: Herbs, Nutrition and Other Holistic Choices;* website is a reliable source of information on safe use of herbs in pregnancy and while breastfeeding from an MD-herbalist; www.AvivaRomm.com.
- Simkin, Penny. *The Birth Partner: A Complete Guide to Childbirth for Dads, Doulas, and All Other Labor Companions, 4th Edition.*
- Tully, Gail. *The Belly Mapping Workbook;* empowers mothers to determine their baby's position in the womb; website contains information for turning babies who are not optimally positioned prior to the birth; www.SpinningBabies.com.
- Weed, Susan. *Wise Woman Herbal for the Childbearing Year; g*ood self-help manual with reliable information for resolving discomforts of pregnancy.

On the Web

- Brennan, Patty, producer. *Yoga and Your Pelvic Floor* (5 videos with Marlene McGrath); YouTube, Center for Childbearing channel.
- Gilliland, Amy. *Doulaing the Doula*. Professional development for the doula blog, http://doulaingthedoula.com/.
- Kim James, https://doulamatch.net/. Free directory listings for doulas.
- Aviva Romm, www.AvivaRomm.com. Website is a reliable source of information on safe use of herbs in pregnancy and while breastfeeding, from an OB/GYN-herbalist; can sign up for her free newsletter.

POWERPOINT SLIDES

INTRODUCTION TO CHILDBIRTH FOR DOULAS

Day 1 ~ DONA Birth Doula Workshop

1

NUTRITION & DISCOMFORTS OF PREGNANCY

2

HORMONES OF LABOR

Oxytocin

Prolactin

Relaxin

Endor-phins

Estrogen

3

Slide 4

OXYTOCIN
- Creates strong, productive contractions
- Letdown of breastmilk
- Enables experience of pleasure
- Maternal behaviors and feelings

RELAXIN
- Relaxes soft tissues, muscles, ligaments and tendons

ESTROGEN
- Decreases pain sensitivity
- Increases intuition

Handwritten note: → governs the whole process of labor... also lets down breastmilk

4

Slide 5

ENDORPHINS
- Morphine-like hormones; reduce pain sensitivity, relax, energize
- Increase with pain and exertion (active labor)
- Help create trance state (withdrawing and instinctual behavior)
- Contribute to euphoric feelings after birth

PROLACTIN
- "Nesting hormone"
- Promotes milk production
- Increases relaxation, ability to bond with baby

5

Slide 6

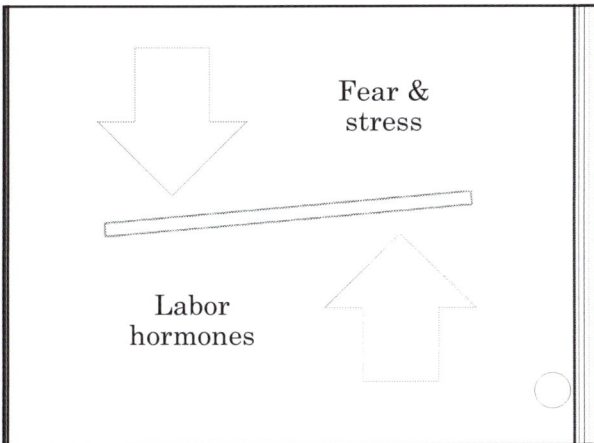

Fear & stress

Labor hormones

6

PHYSIOLOGIC EFFECTS OF FEAR

Fight or Flight

- Activates autonomic nervous system
- Releases stress hormones
- Increases respiration and heart rate, need for O2
- Blood shunted to the extremities

7

NEGATIVE EFFECTS

Hormonal Blocking	MotherBaby
o Increased sensation of pain o Slows contractions o Results in prolonged labor o More fetal distress o Increased use of medical interventions	o Birth experienced as traumatic o Increased risk of PTSD, mood disorders o Adverse effects on bonding & breastfeeding

O2 is shunted away from uterus

8

-labor may stop if fear takes over

Fear

Pain

Tension

9

CONSCIOUS BRAIN VS. PRIMAL BRAIN

The 3 Brains

Neocortex
Human Brain
Logic/Abstract Thought

Limbic System
Mammalian
Emotions/Empathy/Parental

Reptilian Complex
Survival/Reproduction

Stimulation of the neocortex (intellect, reasoning) is counter-productive in labor.

10

- trying to reason through this process "how much longer do I have to do this?"

SUMMARY: ANTAGONISTS TO RELEASE OF OXYTOCIN

➢ Stress hormones
➢ Stimulation of the neocortex

11

Poster Exercise

Brainstorm factors in the labor room that might increase stress hormones or stimulation of the conscious brain in the birthing mother.

Environment
Behavior
Words
People
Events

12

Poster Exercise

Brainstorm factors in the labor room conducive to the release of oxytocin.

Environment
Behavior
Words
People
Events

13

~ Videos ~
Stages of Labor
and
Giving Birth

14

becoming Dona-certified:
- list of resources:
  - chiropractors in the area who know Webster technique
  - whole process from Active labor (6cm) - on

15

DONA INTERNATIONAL BIRTH DOULA WORKSHOP

Day 2

16

WHAT DO DOULAS DO?

Emotional Support

Physical Support

Informational Support

Empowerment

Negotiating Relationships

17

THE MEANING OF SUPPORT

18

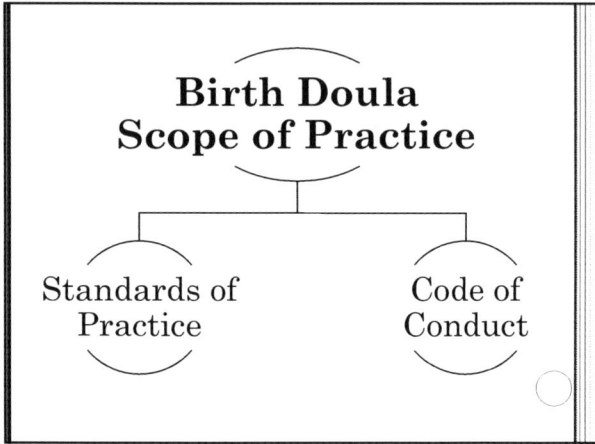

Birth Doula Scope of Practice

Standards of Practice

Code of Conduct

19

SCOPE OF PRACTICE BENEFITS BOTH DOULA AND CLIENT

- ❖ Enhances communication
- ❖ Helps you deliver respectful care
- ❖ Establishes professional boundaries
- ❖ Limits liability

People Boundary

Places Boundary

Time Boundary

20

YOUR CLIENT CONTRACT ...

- o Services provided
- o Limitations
- o Policies regarding backup
- o Timeframe for services
- o Fees and terms of payment
- o Refund policy

- o Responsibilities of each party
- o Signatures (include partner!)

TRANSPARENCY
Good communication of mutual expectations is key!

21

WHAT ADDITIONAL BOUNDARIES MIGHT
YOU SET WITH CLIENTS?

22

DONA INTERNATIONAL
BIRTH DOULA CERTIFICATION

o Value of certification?
o Requirements Q&A
o Re-certification

23

24

25

ACTIVE LABOR

o Contraction pattern?
o Dilation?
o Features?

26

THERE IS A DIFFERENCE BETWEEN PAIN AND SUFFERING

Suffering

Pain

Not okay

Can be managed

27

"GATE CONTROL THEORY OF PAIN" OR "NEUROMATRIX PAIN THEORY"

- Synapses between pain impulses coming from the cervix and the brain
- Spinal cord acts as a "gate"—allows or blocks
- Can be interrupted by sending a different message

- Comfort Measures Checklist, p. 6.3
- See what works
- May change

28

THE THREE R'S = SIGNS OF COPING

Relaxation	Rhythm	Ritual
• Lack of muscle tension, gripping • Lack of "fighting" one's way through	• Movement • Breathing • Sounds • Words	• Combination that works and repeats with each cx • Often spontaneous

29

SO, NOT COPING =

Muscle Tension	Lack of Rhythm	No Ritual
• Do a visual scan from head to feet • Signs of tension?	• What might this look like?	• Sense of dread • Pain not managed • Suffering • Wants to escape • "I don't know what to do with myself."

30

SUPPORT THE RITUAL

Doulas	**Partners**
o Blend with her	o Might be amazing!
o Match her rhythm	o May not know how to help
o Model for partners	o Often have a different rhythm than mom's
o Mom who can't be happy in any position for more than 3 cxs? Her ritual is CHANGE.	

If it's not broke, don't fix it!

31

HYPNOTIC SUGGESTION (P. 5.9)

o You're doing so well.	o Say with me, "I can do it."
o That's it … that's the way	o You're doing exactly what you need to be doing.
o You're doing it!	o Each cx is bringing our baby closer.
o You are so strong.	
o You're working with the contractions so well.	o I'm proud of you.
o You are relaxing beautifully.	o Perfect, just perfect.
o That was a good one!	o Just rest now.
o I'm right here.	o Good, beautiful
o I will help you.	o Just breathe.
o You can do it.	

32

PAIN COPING ~ WATER!

o *Best non-drug pain relief available*

o Full immersion is best

o Support for physical positioning

o Showers work too

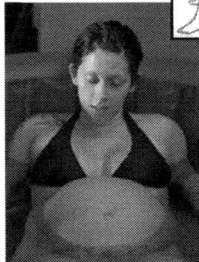

33

VISUALIZATION

o Ride the waves.
o You are a surfer …
o trying not to crash and burn.
o If you wipe out, get back on your board and go again.
o Hypnobirthing classes

34

MANTRA

o Repeating one word or a specific string of words; e.g., "I can do it."
o May overlap with a visualization (e.g., "baby, baby, baby" or "open, open, open")

35

PRESENT MOMENT AWARENESS

o Numbers game
o Anchor her in the present moment
o "Just get through this one."
o "Just rest now."

36

VOCALIZATIONS

- Release the intensity
- Helps to make noise
- Moaning
- Intone a vibration
- "Roar like a mama lion."

37

VOCALIZATIONS ~ GO LOW!

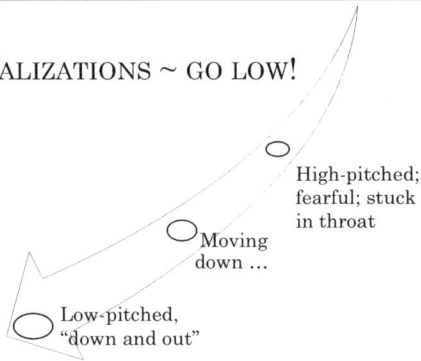

High-pitched; fearful; stuck in throat

Moving down …

Low-pitched, "down and out"

38

TRANSITION ~ THE DOULA'S ROLE

- Signs of transition?
- Move in close
- Moment-to-moment

PANIC BUTTON

39

BENEFITS OF THE PEANUT BALL

- With or without an epidural
- Widens pelvic outlet
- Encourages rotation and descent of baby
- Assists rotation of posterior baby

© M & W Productions

40

Too small = not as effective

Too large = places too much torque causing guarding rather than relaxation

Just right!

41

PEANUT BALL STATISTICS

- Decreases 1st stage by 102–108 mins
- Decreases 2nd stage by 27–29 mins
- Decreases cesarean rates by 12% !!!

42

TOUCH TECHNIQUES

o Hand-holding partner exercise

o Gaining trust and getting in sync

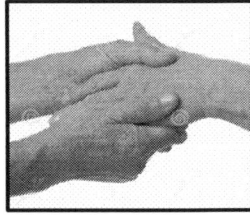

43

EARLY LABOR

Grounding and calming techniques

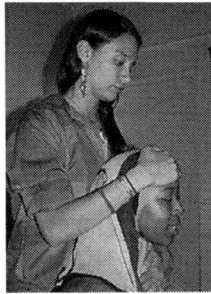

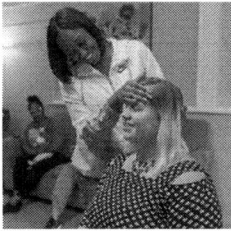

44

ACUPRESSURE FOR LABOR

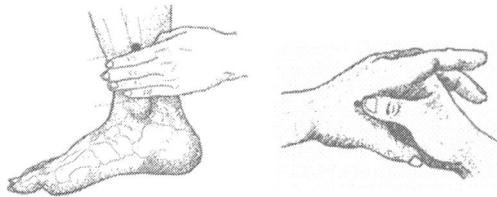

45

DONA International Birth Doula Workshop

Day 3

46

Onset of Labor

- Signs of impending labor?
- 3 ways for labor to begin?
- Timing of cxs?
- Emotions?

47

Needs of the Mother

- Self-care reminders
- Feedback, reassurance
- Relaxation techniques
- Distraction, companion
- Signs she is moving into active labor?
- Communication with doula

48

2ND STAGE OF LABOR

Coached Pushing

Physiologic Pushing

49

PHYSIOLOGIC PUSHING

o Angle (axis of pelvis)
o Gravity

50

2ND STAGE ~ THE DOULA'S ROLE

o Support for normal physiology
o Physical support for positioning
o Encouragement, feedback
o Address fears?
o Comfort measures?

51

PREVENTING PERINEAL TEARS

o Slowing down
- Cease voluntary pushing efforts
- Let uterus do the work

o Breathing vs. pushing

o Panting (not engaging the diaphragm)

Breath holding = Pushing

52

HOW DOULAS CAN HELP

Prenatally	At the Birth
o Encourage client to educate herself	o Remind her at start of 2nd stage about burning sensation
o Encourage communication with care provider	o Help with panting through the burn
o Integrate into birth plan	o **"Breathe with me"**
	o Eye contact if needed
	o Enable hot compresses if desired

53

3RD STAGE

o Skin-to-skin

o Stay engaged with process

o Guidance about what's next

o Support birth plan

54

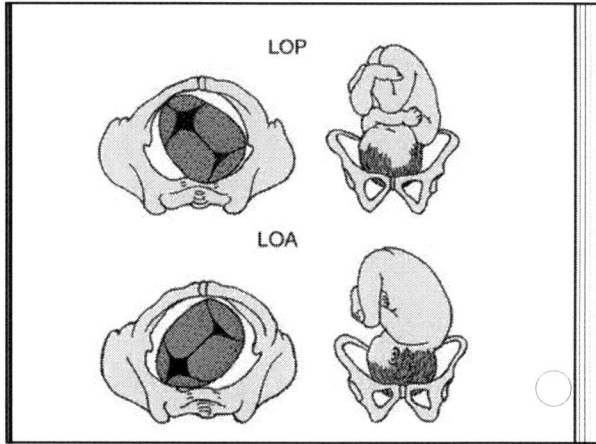

55

FEATURES OF A POSTERIOR PRESENTATION?

- Back PAIN! (intensity)
- Back pain doesn't go away between cxs
- May be long prodromal phase
- Stalled progress ~ 6cm
- Anterior lip of cervix

56

COMPARE ...

Anterior	Posterior

57

WHERE IS THE BABY?

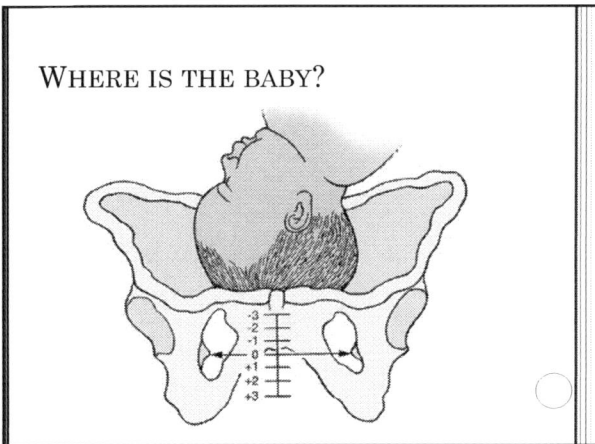

58

THE PELVIS

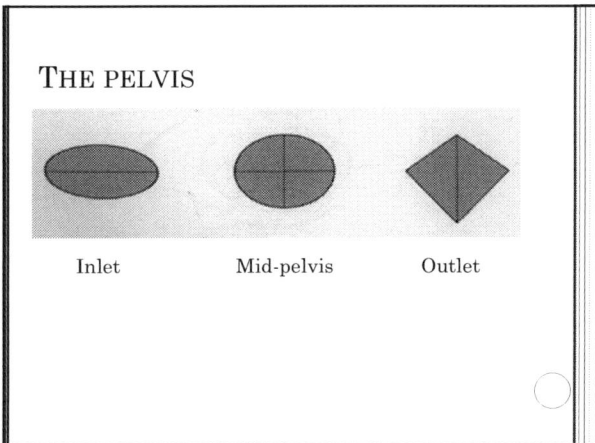

Inlet   Mid-pelvis   Outlet

59

HELP A POSTERIOR BABY ROTATE

Before Labor

o Pelvic rocks
o Chiropractic "Webster technique"
o Diaphragmatic release
o Visualization
o Homeopathy
o TCM (moxibustion)

www.SpinningBabies.com

60

KNEE-CHEST

o Best results before 4cm dilation
o Long prodromal labor? Assume baby is mal-positioned and try knee-chest

61

KNEE-CHEST

o Hold till something changes (may take a couple of hours)
  • Cxs may increase
  • Cxs may stop
  • Take a nap
  • Burst of energy/ manic
  • Emotional catharsis

Bean bag chair might help her stay in position

62

CREATING ASYMMETRY IN PELVIS

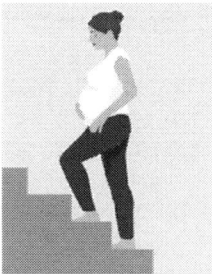

o Hands and knees, one-leg down, one up
o Lunge position
o Lunge with peanut ball
o Switch sides

63

POSTERIOR WITH EPIDURAL & PEANUT BALL

o OP turn every 30–45 min

o OA can let mom rest for 1–2 hours

© M & W Productions.   © M & W Productions.

64

___

PAIN RELIEF FOR POSTERIOR

Counter-pressure on sacrum
- Tennis balls in tube sock
- Pool noodle

65

___

IMMEDIATE POSTPARTUM RECOVERY

o Needs of mother/ baby/partner
o Hospital protocols
o What's happening with mom?
- Stitches?
- Shakes
- Bleeding
- Contractions
- Feed her

o Doula's role during this time

66

THE POSTPARTUM VISIT

What is your purpose?

What assessments are you making?

67

Assessing needs

Processing birth

Saying goodbye

68

THE DOULA'S TOOLS

Voice

Balls, rebozo, etc.

Eye Contact

Energy Spirit Heart

Know-ledge

Hands, Touch

Breath

69

Made in the USA
Monee, IL
20 January 2020